Harry Potter and the Millennials

Harry Potter and the Millennials

Research Methods and the
Politics of the Muggle Generation

ANTHONY GIERZYNSKI
with
KATHRYN EDDY

The Johns Hopkins University Press
Baltimore

© 2013 The Johns Hopkins University Press
All rights reserved. Published 2013
Printed in the United States of America on acid-free paper

2 4 6 8 9 7 5 3 1

The Johns Hopkins University Press
2715 North Charles Street
Baltimore, Maryland 21218-4363
www.press.jhu.edu

Library of Congress Cataloging-in-Publication Data
Gierzynski, Anthony, 1961–
Harry Potter and the Millennials : research methods and the politics of
the Muggle generation / Anthony Gierzynski ; with Kathryn Eddy.
pages cm
Includes bibliographical references and index.
ISBN-13: 978-1-4214-1032-6 (hardcover : alk. paper)
ISBN-13: 978-1-4214-1033-3 (pbk. : alk. paper)
ISBN-13: 978-1-4214-1034-0 (electronic)
ISBN-10: 1-4214-1032-x (hardcover : alk. paper)
ISBN-10: 1-4214-1033-8 (pbk. : alk. paper)
ISBN-10: 1-4214-1034-6 (electronic)
1. Rowling, J. K.—Influence. 2. Generation Y—Political activity. 3. Potter,
Harry (Fictitious character). I. Eddy, Kathryn, 1981– II. Title.
PR6068.O93Z675 2013
823'.914—dc23   2012047014

A catalog record for this book is available from the British Library.

Special discounts are available for bulk purchases of this book.
For more information, please contact Special Sales at 410-516-6936
or specialsales@press.jhu.edu.

The Johns Hopkins University Press uses environmentally friendly book
materials, including recycled text paper that is composed of at least 30
percent post-consumer waste, whenever possible.

For Chay,
and all the magic he has brought into our lives

CONTENTS

We would like to thank all of the University of Vermont students who have contributed to the development of this project. The following University of Vermont students contributed in various ways to the development and implementation of the research that comprises the foundation for this book: Julie Seger, who participated in the design of the original study as part of POLS237, Film, TV and Public Opinion, worked on the expanded sample as part of an independent study and collected qualitative interview data for her honors thesis; Gaurav Pruthi, Ellen Simpson, and Norman Woolworth, who participated in the design of the original study as part of POLS237, Film, TV and Public Opinion, and worked the expanded sample as part of an independent study; Ian Collins, Catherine Dixon, Laura Eddy, Shauneen Grout, Clayton Oberst, Christopher Overton, Gabriela Riley, Stephen Rowe, Ashley Thygesen, and Gordon Whelply, who were involved in the design of the original study as part of POLS237, Film, TV and Public Opinion, in the spring 2009 semester; and Joanna Benjamin, Lindsay Cahill, Dana Christiansen, Zach Clark, Dean LoRusso, Luke Martin, Kofi Mensah, Isaac Moche, Patrick O'Donnell, and Caitlin Perry, who collected interview data as part of the follow-up study in POLS237 in the spring 2010 semester. These students' enthusiasm and hard work helped to make this project possible. We would also like to thank all of the University of Vermont students who have participated in the design and implementation of projects in POLS237—those projects were the precursors to the one published here.

We would also like to thank my colleagues who allowed our survey to be administered in their classes at the University of Vermont and colleagues at other schools who administered the surveys in their classes: Rick Travis and David Breaux at Mississippi State University, Robert Brown at the University of Mississippi, Wendy Johnston at Adirondack Community College, Matt Moore and Anika Leithner at California Polytechnic State University, Matt Potowski at Iowa State University, and Stephen Woolworth at Pacific Lutheran University. We would also like to thank the University of Vermont's Political Science Department staff, Candace Smith and Carol Tank-Day, for help putting together and mailing the survey material for this study. We would thank all our friends and family for their support, interest in this project, and encouragement, including John Dietz for organizing the Thursday night book club at the Three Penny Taproom and all of my teammates on the Montpelier Monties of the Vermont Men's Senior Baseball League.

Finally, we thank the anonymous peer reviewers for their very helpful feedback on this manuscript. We are grateful to all of those at the Johns Hopkins University Press for their support and work on this project.

This book is dedicated to our most wonderful son, Chay, whom we love right up to the end of the universe and back. We hope you are able to find some of the magic in this world.

Harry Potter and the Millennials

Isn't It Just a Story?

J. K. Rowling's Harry Potter series has had a powerful effect on the Millennial Generation.[1] Hundreds of millions of Millennials grew up captivated by the world of the boy wizard—they read the books, attended midnight book-release parties (many dressed as the characters), watched the movies, and joined the Harry Potter fan community. By the time the seventh and final book in the series was released, the first six books had already sold more than 325 million copies, many of which were read multiple times by their owners. The seventh book set the record for most books sold in the United States in twenty-four hours—8.3 million.[2] Seven of the eight movies based on the books are in the twenty-three top-grossing films of all time worldwide (the eighth, *Harry Potter and the Prisoner of Azkaban*, is number thirty-two).[3] The popularity of the books and movies led Universal Studios to open the Wizarding World of Harry Potter, a twenty-acre fully immersive theme park at its Orlando location where fans can experience the town of Hogsmeade and sample butterbeer, go into Ollivander's to be chosen by a wand, journey inside Hogwarts Castle, and ride a hippogriff or a dragon.

Additional indications of the extent of fan engagement can be found on popular Internet sites such as Mugglenet.com and The Leaky Cauldron (http://www.the-leaky-cauldron.org/). A short time spent on these sites reveals the levels at which many fans are devoted to the series. Fans not only post news and discuss the latest developments about Harry Potter, but they also create and post Harry Potter–inspired fan fiction, art, and videos; download video games; share recipes; and buy Harry Potter merchandise (including Bertie Bott's Every Flavor Beans and other various candy items eaten by the characters). Fans have created Mugglespace.com, their own Harry Potter social network. They even have their own Harry Potter music, played by Wizard Rock bands. And, finally, while their broomsticks never really leave the ground, more than three hundred colleges and high schools around the world now actually have Quidditch teams.[4]

Beyond its evident popularity, however, little is known about specific ways the Harry Potter books and movies have affected its main audience, the Millennial Generation. Rowling did not set out to write a political tale; however, her story is imbued with values, perspectives, characters, and lessons that may have influenced the political views of the generation that grew up in the Potter world.[5] Could the series have had anything to do with the fact that two-thirds of the Millennials in the United States voted for Barack Obama in 2008?[6] Could the series be partly responsible for the generally liberal values and views that the Millennials voice in public opinion polls?[7] The typical first reaction to such questions regarding the effect of the Harry Potter series on its fans is to assert that it is just a story. But no story is "just a story." As most cultures recognize, stories are powerful and necessary vehicles for learning cultural values and perspectives. Even the "news" from which we expect to learn what is going on in the world is told *in stories*. All stories we read or watch unfold, or those that are told to us, whether for fun or to obtain information, invariably contain lessons—messages, warnings, maxims—we internalize and characters whose traits we admire and emulate or characters we despise and don't wish to be like at all. It doesn't matter whether the stories are fictional or factual, or whether the stories take place in a realistic or fantasy setting. After all, "[h]aven't Luke Skywalker and Santa Claus affected your lives more than most real people . . . ? I mean, whether Jesus is real or not, he . . . he's had a bigger impact on the world than any of us have. And the same could be said of Bugs Bunny and, a-and Superman and Harry Potter. They've changed my life, changed the way I act on the Earth."[8]

As Kyle Broflovski (a character from the television show *South Park*) so eloquently put it in the above quote, some of these fictional or mythical characters and their narratives are such a huge part of our culture that they can't help but affect us. Ronald Moore, a writer of the critically acclaimed television show *Battlestar Galactica*, testified to this point in an op-ed piece in the *New York Times* about the influence of the *Star Trek* television series on him growing up. "*Star Trek* would literally change my life. . . . *Star Trek* painted a noble, heroic vision of the future, and that vision became my lodestar. As I grew into adolescence, the show provided a handy reference against which to judge the questions that my young mind began to ask: What is the obligation of a free society toward the less fortunate? Does an 'advanced' culture have the right to spread its ideas among more 'primitive' ones? What does it mean to be human, and at what point do we lose our humanity to our technology?"[9]

Popular culture is rife with television shows, movies, books, video games that we immerse ourselves in, that invariably contain stories and characters with lessons and values that affect how we see the world, including how we see the world politically. In these stories, the characters learn a wide variety of politically relevant lessons. Included among those could be lessons regarding the role of violence when faced with hardship; the value of equality; the struggles of good versus evil; the impact of technology on society; the pros and cons of religion and belief; the value of following the rules or breaking them; notions of destiny and free will; the desirability of waiting for individual heroes or, conversely, seeing the need to get involved, pull together with others, and do something ourselves; the dangers or rewards of revenge and forgiveness; and so on. Though obviously learned by the characters, these lessons often end up informing us—as well as shaping how we view the world. This is especially true if we identify with characters who become models through which values and character traits may be acquired.[10]

Despite the potential effect of stories and characters on the political views of those exposed to them, social scientists have not devoted much attention to the ways fictional stories can affect people's political views.[11] Notable exceptions in the political science literature include studies finding effects of the 1980s made-for-television movie *The Day After*, the 1980s television miniseries *Amerika*, the effect of an environmental docudrama on attitude construction, and the influence of *The Daily Show*.[12] Outside political science, media effects research has focused most heavily on the impact of the portrayal of violence and sex, bad behaviors (such as smoking), and the impact of media portrayals on stereotypes, with infrequent attempts to connect such findings to subjects' political perspectives.[13] We know from this latter research that fictional portrayals can affect people's attitudes and behavior in general, so why wouldn't it affect their politics as well? This broad question represents the context for our more specific queries regarding the effects of the Harry Potter series.

Some characters and their stories seem to engage generation after generation. The Star Wars saga, for example, seems to have had a lasting effect on successive generations, starting with Gen Xers, who saw the first movies in the theaters in the late 1970s and early 1980s, to the five- to ten-year-olds who are just now being drawn in by the Star Wars Lego sets and cartoon series (our six-year-old among them . . . the Legos, not the cartoons). The Lord of the Rings engrossed the baby boomers and early Gen Xers as books and then drew in Millennials with the blockbuster movie versions; the additional movies based on *The Hobbit* will no doubt draw in the next generation. Going back further in time one can identify movies, television shows, and books that were so popular that they not only became part of the culture when they first appeared but continue to be referenced today—think *Casablanca, All in the Family, The Catcher in the Rye, M*A*S*H, The Graduate,* and so forth. In the 1980s and 1990s many of these classics were alluded to in television shows (including cartoons), so without ever having viewed *Casablanca,* one of us knew many of the movie's familiar lines and their contexts within our society; the same sort of referencing continues now, as popular stories become further mortared into the foundations of our culture. Jon Stewart of *The Daily Show* and Stephen Colbert of *The Colbert Report* can't help but make at least one reference to Star Wars a week on their popular political satire shows. And, lest you think this is just a phenomenon of popular culture as opposed to political culture, remember that Ronald Reagan called for a "Star Wars" program that would develop space-based interceptors of nuclear missiles, and he called the Soviet Union the "evil empire" after it destroyed a commercial Korean airliner. It is not just movie-actor-turned-presidents who use such references. Indeed, and apropos the topic of this book, labeling an opponent as Voldemort (or a supporter of Voldemort) has become rather popular in the wake of the Harry Potter series, as an Internet search of news outlets will quickly demonstrate. A lighter illustration of this can be found on the YouTube video depicting Voldemort endorsing Rick Perry, candidate for the Republican 2012 presidential nomination. Popular entertainment has become so ingrained in our culture and in our politics that it only makes sense it would play a role in how citizens see politics and government.

While the stories in our entertainment media can affect generation after generation, some stories, because of their timing, have their largest effect on one single generation. The Harry Potter story, which exploded onto the cultural scene just when the Millennial Generation was gaining awareness of the political world, is one such phenomenon. While the story of Harry Potter may continue to affect subsequent generations, its biggest impact will likely have been on the generation that experienced the series while growing up during the ten plus years the series literally dominated the culture. Given this potentially large effect on Millennials we have focused our research and devoted this book to the research question of the impact of Harry Potter on the politics of the Millennial Generation.

We are not claiming or implying that J. K. Rowling intentionally tried to teach or influence her readers politically in any way. This book is not about some liberal conspiracy to brainwash the youth of the world. What we are arguing is simply that all stories inherently contain lessons and characters we wish to emulate regardless of the intent of the author. As all stories invariably reflect an author's perspectives, so the telling of Harry Potter likely grew out of Rowling's experience and knowledge and not necessarily from any overt attempt to persuade those who would read and become captivated by the "boy who lived." Beyond the inadvertent contributions from the perspectives and experiences of authors, lessons may also be buried within stories simply due to the nature of storytelling itself— the demands of the narrative or the nature of the genre, for example—or because of cultural factors that shape the stories our authors tell. So, whether J. K. Rowling was out to influence a generation—an intent we sincerely doubt that she had—is of no concern to us. The point is that her story, like that of any other storyteller, was filled with values, perspectives, and characters that had the potential to shape the values and perspectives of those who read or listened to it, and, unlike any other recent storyteller, Rowling and her Harry Potter saga gripped worldwide audiences, pervading the lives of the Millennial Generation who grew from grade schoolers to adults over the course of the ten years her books were released.

So what impact did a generation's growing up as fans of Harry Potter have on that generation's politics? And how does one find evidence for such an effect? These questions and the broader question regarding entertainment media's effects on politics are what motivated the work on this book. Within these pages we discuss the way we went about searching for political effects of the tale of the boy who lived, issues involved in uncovering evidence of media effects such as those of the Harry Potter series, and what we discovered.

In short, we found that Harry Potter fans tend to be more accepting of those who are different, to be more politically tolerant, to be more supportive of equality, to be less authoritarian, to be more opposed to the use of violence and torture, to be less cynical, and to evince a higher level of political efficacy. They are also more liberal, with a more negative view of the Bush years, and as noted earlier, they are more likely to have voted for Barack Obama for president. This is not to say that all Harry Potter fans have these traits (or all nonfans lack them); what we are saying is that Potter fans are more likely to exhibit these perspectives that parallel the lessons and character traits prominent in the series. The differences between fans and nonfans remain even when controlling for, or factoring out, other known predictors (key among them whether the subjects were avid readers). In all, our findings suggest that the Harry Potter phenomenon had an independent and multifaceted effect on the politics of the Millennial Generation (both direct and indirect). While our findings are highly suggestive of a Harry Potter effect (especially when combined with the theoretical arguments from political socialization, generations, and media effects), we cannot, as our discussion of methodological issues involved in such research makes clear, definitively prove that the Harry Potter series *caused* Millennial fans to be politically different from nonfans. So, ultimately we hope this work inspires readers to tackle the methodological issues of measuring entertainment media's political effects in order to determine whether there is additional evidence to support the idea that popular entertainment media, like the Harry Potter series, help to shape our political perspectives.

Outline of the Book

Before discussing the research from which the above findings were gathered, we must detail the politically relevant lessons of the Harry Potter series. Examining the series with a political eye reveals that the tale of the boy wizard is rich with content that has the potential to shape readers' political views. One such politically relevant lesson repeated throughout the Harry Potter series is the value of accepting those who may appear different and even frightening. Identifying, sympathizing, and connecting with the heroes of the books means relating to characters who accept and even befriend half-giants (Hagrid), werewolves (Professor Lupin), and house-elves (Dobby)—all of whom, even in the wizarding world, are considered inferior, dangerous, or both and are largely ignored or actively shunned and discriminated against. It also means being in conflict with those who do discriminate based on such differences. For example, in the earlier books, Harry's main antagonist is another boy, one from a privileged and so-called pure-blood family, Draco Malfoy, who casually voices views akin to racial purity for wizards (including weeding out all those who have been tainted by Muggle or nonwizard blood). Draco also maliciously demeans Harry's friend Hermione with the wizarding world's equivalent to a racial epithet, "mudblood." Conversely, revered characters, such as Hogwarts's headmaster Dumbledore (an exceptionally powerful and honored wizard), are shown to be extremely accepting and open-minded; Dumbledore employs and trusts a werewolf and half-giant and even extends amnesty to a known associate of the evil Lord Voldemort. The levels of political tolerance that follow from this acceptance of diversity are interesting, as are specific lessons about political tolerance (such as whether any but pure-bloods should be accepted for instruction at Hogwarts School for Witchcraft and Wizardry, where the bulk of the series is set).

The lesson that conformity and strict obedience toward authority—values that are at the heart of the authoritarian predisposition—are destructive also appears frequently throughout the series.[14] The story's antagonists insist on conformity (like Harry's neglectful guardians the Dursleys or those wizards within Voldemort's ranks), and some show obedience and subservience to the powerful even in situations that call for dissent (the Death Eaters to Lord Voldemort and Dolores Umbridge to the ministry, for example).

The series very clearly demonstrates that violence and torture are the devices of "bad guys" and cannot be justified, even as a last resort. The protagonists avoid violence and abhor torture; the antagonists use them freely. Harry refuses to use the "killing curse" even against the ultimate bad guy, Voldemort, and is known by most wizards, good and bad, for simply trying to disarm his opponents as opposed to harming them. The one time Harry strays from his nonviolent nature helps illustrate this point. In the anguished moments after witnessing his godfather's murder, Harry attempts the torture curse against the killer, Death Eater Bellatrix Lestrange. The attempt fails and Lestrange mocks Harry. "Never used an Unforgivable Curse before, have you, boy? . . . You need to *mean* them, Potter! You need to really want to cause pain—to enjoy it—righteous anger won't hurt me for long."[15]

Other politically relevant content includes the treatment of the wizarding world's Ministry of Magic, a government whose leaders are portrayed as bumbling, paranoid about losing power, and incompetent or corrupt; lessons in skepticism and how people or creatures are not always what they seem; and, finally, lessons about controlling one's own fate and the need to work with others in order to defeat adversaries. Chapter 1 focuses on these areas and provides a brief overview of the Harry Potter world for those who are unfamiliar with it.

Revealing politically relevant content within the Harry Potter series is one thing; showing how these aspects of the story affect readers is a whole other matter. How could all the politically relevant lessons of the Harry Potter series have affected its fans? The answer lies in the fact that our political perspectives and values are not programmed into our DNA; instead we acquire political values and views from our culture. We learn how to act and what to value in our society from people—our families and our friends or members of our community—and institutions—schools, religious institutions, and the media (television, video games, movies, and books). From our preteen years to our adolescence, when we are just becoming aware of the political world and forming our initial impressions, these agents can have a tremendous impact on the values and outlooks that form the basis of our politics. The Millennial Generation became engrossed in Harry Potter at just this time in their political socialization, heightening the potential impact and making it so that the tales from the wizarding world may have had a significant impact on shaping the nature of their generation. Chapter 2 elaborates on the process of political socialization, takes a fuller look at the Millennial Generation and other developments that helped to determine their politics, and explores other means by which a work of fiction may lead fans to adopt certain values, attitudes, and predispositions.

Once the routes to possible influence are covered we turn to the search for actual evidence that connects Harry Potter to the politics of fans within the Millennial Generation. In chapters 3 and 4, we report research findings on the effect of the Harry Potter series and the methodological issues involved in uncovering such evidence. That research includes a survey of 1,141 college students from around the United States and the testimony of Harry Potter fans themselves. Chapter 3 explores the differences between Harry Potter fans and nonfans, finding that fans display values and perspectives that parallel those of the Harry Potter series. But that begs the question, which came first, these views or becoming a fan of Harry Potter? Did the books cause fans to adopt these views or did the Millennials become fans because they (or their parents) already held such views? That the Harry Potter series was so widely read and that Millennials were exposed to its lessons and characters at their most politically vulnerable age, suggests that at least part of the differences between fans and nonfans is due to Millennials becoming so engaged in the series. Chapter 4 addresses this issue empirically, reporting on analyses that attempt to ascertain the degree to which the tales of the boy wizard affected the political perspective of Millennials once other known predictors of such perspectives are controlled for.

What does it all mean? What are the implications regarding the political impact of Harry Potter beyond its effect on the Millennial Generation? Since the Harry Potter series seems to have helped to shape the politics of Millennials, what impact might *The Hunger Games*, *Avatar*, the *Twilight* saga, *Star Wars*, or other widely consumed media have (or have had) on other generations? What are the political ramifications of the consumption of such media on school-aged children, who will spend more hours in front of a television than in the classroom upon graduation?[16] And how do we go about measuring and testing for such effects? The last chapter will wrap up these discussions, placing Harry Potter and the wizarding world into the larger context of popular culture's role in the formation of our politics.

CHAPTER ONE

The Subtle (and Not-So-Subtle) Political Lessons of Harry Potter

To best understand the wealth of political material present in the Harry Potter series, a basic introduction to the story is necessary. Readers experience the wizarding world from the perspective of Harry Potter, an orphaned boy living with his nonmagical aunt and uncle, Petunia and Vernon Dursley, and their son, Dudley. Harry grows up unhappy and neglected by the Dursley family; he is unaware of his magical powers (though his guardians are painfully aware) and oblivious of his fame in the wizarding world. When Harry was just an infant, Lord Voldemort, the most infamous dark wizard of his age, murdered his parents. On the night of their death, Harry miraculously survived the Killing Curse, Avada Kedavra—one of the three so-called Unforgivable Curses—which Voldemort attempted on Harry after performing it on Harry's pleading mother. For reasons unknown, the spell rebounded to Voldemort and destroyed him. As the only person to ever survive and stop the wrath of Lord Voldemort, Harry is internationally known as "the boy who lived" and celebrated throughout the wizarding world as Voldemort's vanquisher. At age eleven, Harry is informed of his magical background and invited to attend Hogwarts School of Witchcraft and Wizardry, the main setting for much of the series. We are introduced to a host of characters both within Hogwarts Castle and in the wizarding world. As the story unfolds, we learn about the ins and outs of this new world along with Harry.

An important tenet under which all wizards in the world of Harry Potter live is the Statute of Secrecy, a Ministry of Magic (wizarding government) law that shields the magical world from exposure to the real world and nonmagical people or Muggles. Lord Voldemort and his followers, the Death Eaters—many of whom remained either locked away, in hiding, or at the very least treated with some suspicion during the ten years that Voldemort was assumed dead—desire an overthrow of the Statute of Secrecy. They wish to rule the Muggles and any other creatures in the world (house-elves, centaurs, werewolves, giants, goblins, and the like, whom they see as inferior slaves) and to assert the superiority of pure-blood wizards over those whose blood has been "muddied" by nonmagical ancestors.

Harry befriends two classmates in the beginning of the series, Ron Weasley and Hermione Granger. Ron and Harry become fast friends, and Ron's family becomes Harry's wizarding foster family. Ron's grandmother was from a prominent pure-blood family and in marrying a Weasley (who was not a pure-blood) was considered a blood-traitor and disowned. Ron's father, Arthur, is employed by the ministry in a low-paying job (which he loves) in the Misuse of Muggle Artifacts Office and has an affinity for Muggles. Hermione is a Muggle-born witch, a magical person born to two nonmagical parents, a trait she shares with Harry's mother. She is incredibly gifted and smart and a tremendous asset to Harry in his adventures throughout the series. That Harry should choose two such characters as his good friends indicates his natural proclivity to put himself in opposition to the views espoused by Voldemort and his followers, which continues throughout the series. Again and again we see Harry surrounding himself with good-hearted wizarding misfits and setting himself against the racist convictions of the Death Eaters.

We are also introduced to two important staff members at Hogwarts: Albus Dumbledore and Severus Snape. Dumbledore is Hogwarts's headmaster and "considered by many [as] the greatest wizard of modern times."[1] Snape is the Potions Master who would much prefer to be teaching classes in defense against the dark arts. His hatred for Harry is undisguised and his former affiliation with the Death Eaters is the source of much doubt among Harry and his friends and allies; Dumbledore, however, remains steadfast in trusting Snape.

Dozens more characters and many adventures line Harry's path through the series, and it is the way Harry and his friends navigate and respond to their many challenges that teaches readers critical life lessons, of which we have selected some of the most politically relevant and most recurrent.

Lesson 1: Diversity and Acceptance; or, Don't Judge People (or Creatures) by Their Appearance or Blood

A consistent lesson throughout the books and movies is acceptance of those who are different from ourselves. Again and again, whether it is ignoring status as a pure-blood to judge individuals on the quality of their character, or simple courtesy toward any person or creature regardless of their appearance or societal position, the tale of the boy wizard teaches that to be good is to reserve judgment, to be open to those who are different. It could be argued that for Harry this tolerance comes easily because the wizarding world is alien to him. Why would he know any better? Yet, as each year passes at Hogwarts and as Harry understands more about his true identity and his place in the larger struggle of good versus evil, he learns he is not alone in accepting and tolerating others, or in his conviction that there are a great many things that need to be changed. The other characters in the story with whom we tend to sympathize, who are painted as reasonable and worthwhile and who offer Harry the support and guidance through his many struggles and battles, are the characters who are most likely to remind us that a book should not be judged by its cover. By contrast, the stories' antagonists are often quick to make judgments and be quite vocal in their bigotry. Draco Malfoy, for example, espouses his intolerant beliefs when he and Harry meet for the first time:

> "You'll soon find out some wizarding families are much better than others, Potter. You don't want to go making friends with the wrong sort. I can help you there."
>
> He held out his hand to shake Harry's, but Harry didn't take it.
>
> "I think I can tell who the wrong sort are for myself, thanks," he said coolly.
>
> "I'd be careful if I were you Potter," Malfoy said slowly. "Unless you're a bit politer you'll go the same way as your parents. They didn't know what was good for them, either. You hang around with riffraff like the Weasleys and that Hagrid, and it'll rub off on you."[2]

Though it isn't necessarily obvious from the beginning of Rowling's tale, the fundamental conflict in the Harry Potter series is racially driven. Draco's prejudice is shared by all those who support Voldemort; their elitism and hatred for anything "non-Wizard" (Muggles or other creatures) is shown first by voicing very publicly their attitudes and beliefs and later by the persecution and imprisonment—and more drastically the torture and murder—of those who they consider "different." "Many of our oldest family trees become a little diseased over time," Voldemort tells Bellatrix. "You must prune yours, must you not, to keep it healthy? Cut away those parts that threaten the health of the rest. . . . And in your family, so in the world . . . we shall cut away the canker that infects us until only those of the true blood remain."[3]

By contrast, sentient magical creatures, such as house-elves, centaurs, and goblins offer readers a variety of eccentric, charming characters that are generally framed as "good." Harry finds comfort and love in several characters who are discriminated against or outwardly hated in wizarding society: his godfather, Sirius Black, is a suspected murderer; his great friend and often protector, Rubeus Hagrid, is a half-giant; his favorite teacher and mentor, who was also a friend of Harry's father, is Remus Lupin, a werewolf.

Harry's penchant for befriending or respecting those who are considered different earns him equal respect from them. He is revered by the house-elf Dobby, whom Harry frees from servitude early on in the series. In the final book, Harry pays Dobby the ultimate tribute by digging and marking a grave for him after his death. This act is witnessed by a goblin named Griphook and in the conversation that ensues we observe both the history of wizard oppression of other creatures, as well as the protagonists—Harry, Ron, and Hermione—demonstrating their attitude of acceptance for *all* kinds of beings:

> "If there was a wizard of whom I would believe that they did not seek personal gain," said Griphook finally, "it would be you, Harry Potter. Goblins and elves are not used to the protection or the respect that you have shown this night. Not from wand-carriers. The right to carry a wand," said the Goblin quietly, "has long been contested between wizards and goblins. . . . As the Dark Lord becomes ever more powerful, your race is set still more firmly above mine! Gringotts falls under Wizarding rule, house-elves are slaughtered, and who amongst the wand-carriers protests?"

"We do!" said Hermione. "We protest! And I'm hunted quite as much as any goblin or elf, Griphook! I'm a Mudblood! . . . Mudblood, and proud of it! I've got no higher position under this new order than you have, Griphook!"[4]

This lesson of acceptance of those who are different is so ubiquitous throughout the books and films that one can't help but expect that fans of the series would internalize such lessons, and from that acceptance, adopt the lessons of tolerance and equality as well.

Lesson 2: Political Tolerance and Equality; or, Everyone Has the Same Rights to Dignity and Freedom

Before they actually meet at Hogwarts, Draco Malfoy and Harry exchange words in a robes shop, and very quickly Draco sneers about the students from nonwizarding families: "I really don't think they should let the other sort in, do you? They're just not the same, they've never been brought up to know our ways. Some of them have never even heard of Hogwarts until they get the letter, imagine. I think they should keep it in the old wizarding families."[5] The conversation is cut short, but we've heard enough to know that some wizards clearly believe they are superior to others and therefore deserve privileges, such as education, that the others do not.

In the second book, we learn a bit more about Hogwarts, its history, and how issues of tolerance and equality divide the school as they had divided its founders. We have already been informed that "there's not a witch or wizard who went bad that wasn't in Slytherin," one of the four "houses" students are sorted into their first year—Ravenclaw, Gryffindor, Hufflepuff, and Slytherin, named for the four founders of Hogwarts and based on their respective qualities as wizards.[6] Students sorted into Slytherin possess cunning; those in Gryffindor, bravery and courage; those in Hufflepuff, loyalty; and those in Ravenclaw, intelligence. Harry, upon hearing Hagrid's statement, desperately wants to be in any house but Slytherin, and despite the traits that could allow him to be sorted into that house, he is also a good candidate for Gryffindor. Regarding the history of the houses, "For a few years, the founders [of Hogwarts] worked in harmony together, seeking out youngsters who showed signs of magic and bringing them to the castle to be educated. But then disagreements sprang up between them. A rift began to grow between Slytherin and the others. Slytherin wished to be more *selective* about the students admitted to Hogwarts. He believed that magical learning should be kept within all-magic families. He disliked taking students of Muggle parentage, believing them to be untrustworthy. After a while there was a serious argument on the subject between Slytherin and Gryffindor, and Slytherin left the school."[7]

Following this rift, Slytherin supposedly placed an evil creature, a basilisk, in a hidden chamber deep within Hogwarts that could only be opened by his heir; when it was free, the creature would purge the school of all those unworthy to study therein. Indeed, it was rumored to have been opened fifty years prior, with one fatality, a young girl considered a mudblood. Though the chamber has never been found, Harry and his friends discover it has been recently opened and that Voldemort (Slytherin's heir) is behind the opening of the chamber in both cases. The first time around he did it himself when he was a student named Tom Riddle; in Harry's time, Voldemort did it by possessing Ginny Weasley, who had been given a diary that turned out to house a fraction of Voldemort's soul.

The denial of basic dignity and freedom to others (in other words, the rejection of tolerance and equality) is not limited to the most evil character in the series. What has clearly been the product of ages of status quo, the Fountain of Magical Brethren in the Ministry of Magic depicts the basic attitude of wizards toward other magical creatures. This is how it was described during Harry's first visit to the ministry: "Halfway down the hall was a fountain. A group of golden statues, larger than life-size, stood in the middle of the circular pool. Tallest of them all was a noble-looking wizard with his wand pointing straight up in the air. Grouped around him were a beautiful witch, a centaur, a goblin, and a house-elf. The last three were all looking adoringly up at the witch and wizard."[8] Magical creatures are considered inferior; they *are* denied their freedom, dignity, and use of magic—no other creature (goblins, centaurs, house-elves, etc.) may carry or use wands, and house-elves, who, it is said, have natural inclinations toward servitude, are treated as slaves and abused by the rich pure-blood families who own them. Harry, on the other hand, not only treats the seemingly mean-spirited house-elf Dobby with respect but frees him from his abusive family. Hermione actually forms an advocacy group on behalf of house-elves, the Society for the Promotion of Elfish Welfare (with the unfortunate acronym S.P.E.W.), whose "short-term aims . . . are to secure house-elves fair wages and working conditions. Our long-term aims include changing the law about non-wand use, and trying to get an elf into the Department for the Regulation and Control of Magical Creatures, because they're shockingly underrepresented."[9]

Lessons of equality also extend to differences in wealth and status. As mentioned earlier, Harry's friend Ron Weasley is looked down upon by many in the story because his family is large and his father doesn't make much money at his ministry job; he is constantly in hand-me-down robes or using previously owned wands and broomsticks.

> "Well, well, well—Arthur Weasley."
>
> It was Mr. Malfoy. He stood with his hand on Draco's shoulder, sneering. . . .
>
> "Lucius," said Mr. Weasley, nodding coldly.
>
> "Busy time at the Ministry, I hear," said Mr. Malfoy. "All those raids . . . I hope they're paying you overtime?"
>
> [Lucius Malfoy] reached into Ginny's cauldron and extracted . . . a very old, very battered copy of *A Beginner's Guide to Transfiguration*. "Obviously not," Mr. Malfoy said. "Dear me, what's the use of being a disgrace to the name of wizard if they don't even pay you well for it?"
>
> . . . "We have a very different idea of what disgraces the name of wizard, Malfoy."
>
> "Clearly," said Mr. Malfoy, his pale blue eyes straying to [the Muggles] Mr. and Mrs. Granger, who were watching apprehensively. "The company you keep, Weasley . . . and I thought your family could sink no lower."[10]

Regardless of their lower class status, the Weasleys are portrayed as good and noble characters that treat Harry and Hermione as part of the family and indeed sacrifice much for Harry and his cause.

Voldemort and his followers not only disdain all who are not purebloods but also think that *only* pure-blood wizards deserve all the rights and privileges of society. Mudbloods, Muggles, and all the rest of the magical creatures are deemed second-class citizens at best. "For those of you who do not know, we are joined here tonight by Charity Burbage, who, until recently, taught at Hogwarts School of Witchcraft and Wizardry . . . Yes . . . Professor Burbage taught the children of witches and wizards all about Muggles . . . how they are not so different from us. . . . Not content with corrupting and polluting the minds of Wizarding children, last week Professor Burbage wrote an impassioned defense of Mudbloods in the *Daily Prophet.* Wizards, she says, must accept these thieves of their knowledge and magic. The dwindling of the purebloods is, says Professor Burbage, a most desirable circumstance. . . . She would have us all mate with Muggles . . . or, no doubt, werewolves. . . ."[11] Voldemort ends this speech by killing Charity Burbage. He and his followers lack even the most basic respect for any life. They take inequality beyond simply not extending the same rights and privileges to all magical creatures; they determine that even the lives of those who would defend the "inferior" are forfeit.

As Voldemort and his followers gain power over the Ministry of Magic in the final books they begin to implement what are in effect ethnic-cleansing policies. They interrogate and force the registration of all witches and wizards with Muggle heritage and strip them of their wizarding privileges. They imprison those who resist. And they further subjugate magical creatures.

Ultimately, Voldemort wishes to exercise domination over Muggles as well, who, for most of the books, are kept in the dark about the parallel magical world. This is perhaps best depicted by the change in the statue in the atrium of the Ministry of Magic once Voldemort's influence waxes, from golden fountain supposedly representing magical creatures in harmony to

a gigantic statue of black stone. . . . It was rather frightening, this vast sculpture of a witch and wizard sitting on ornately carved thrones. . . . Engraved in foot-high letters at the base of the statue were the words MAGIC IS MIGHT. . . .

Harry looked more closely and realized that what he had thought were decoratively carved thrones were actually mounds of carved humans: hundreds and hundreds of naked bodies, men, women, and children, all with rather stupid, ugly faces, twisted and pressed together to support the weight of the handsomely robed wizards.[12]

In the Harry Potter world, the protagonists are constantly objecting to, and fighting against, these injustices that deprive classes of individuals their rights, equal treatment, and freedoms while it is the antagonists who continually practice intolerance and evince the companion disposition of authoritarianism.

Lesson 3: Don't Be an Authoritarian Git

Following World War II and the destruction of the Nazi regime, those who studied politics and society set about to understand the nature of persons who would support fascist regimes. In the process, they developed a theory that there were certain personality types—authoritarian personalities—that were prone to following authority regardless of the morality of the actions (as most famously illustrated in the Milgram experiments in which subjects thought they were inflicting excruciating pain through electric shocks).[13] This antidemocratic personality was also associated with bigotry and intolerance of those who were deemed as being inferior. Due to limitations with the research, this notion of an authoritarian personality was dropped until Karen Stenner reconceptualized authoritarianism as a personality *dynamic* in her book *The Authoritarian Dynamic*. Stenner conceived of the authoritarian dynamic as a product of a stable individual predisposition that is activated by fears engendered by political dissent and diversity, "moral decay," social disorder, and national decline. Authoritarian fears are alleviated by defense of the collective normative order: positive differentiation of the in-group, devaluation and discrimination against out-groups, obedience to authorities, conformity to rules and norms, and intolerance and punishment of those who fail to obey and conform.[14]

Many of the antagonists in the Harry Potter series provide perfect illustrations of the authoritarian dynamic Stenner described. It is evident in Harry's uncle, Vernon Dursley. Uncle Vernon is extremely concerned about appearing "normal" (conformity seeking), narrow-minded, intolerant of the magical, and in favor of harsh punishment, especially when his "normal" world is threatened, which, with Harry around, is pretty much all the time. For many years, Harry's bedroom was a closet under the stairs, and his uncle always tried to keep him hidden so he wouldn't ruin the appearance of his "normal" family.

The Malfoy family offers another example. As servants of the Dark Lord, they are Harry's most apparent and immediate enemies. Draco and Harry clash from their first encounters, and Draco's father, Lucius, is responsible for passing along Voldemort's diary to Ginny Weasley. They are extremely prejudiced against anyone deemed beneath them—Mudbloods, Muggles, the Weasley family, and magical creatures (Dobby was their house-elf until Harry tricked Lucius into freeing him).

But perhaps the best manifestation of authoritarianism in the series is Dolores Umbridge. Umbridge is a pivotal ministry character in the fifth book; she is thoroughly loyal to the Minister of Magic, Cornelius Fudge (who is a perfect illustration of lesson 5), and intent on discrediting and controlling Dumbledore and Harry. A stickler for the rules, she loathes part-humans, thirsts for power, and remains an unflinching follower no matter who is in power above her. Umbridge's character is easily despicable—her demeanor and actions are thoroughly obnoxious to readers. She takes over as instructor for Defense against the Dark Arts at Hogwarts, and in the classroom she institutes strict discipline and focuses on rote memorization, diminishing her students' potential to learn anything of value. "Wands away and quills out, please."[15] Her "carefully structured, theory-centered, Ministry-approved course of defensive magic" involves students not actually learning about and practicing dueling and defense against the dark arts but reading about the principles underlying such spells.[16] Umbridge institutes this curriculum because her boss, Fudge, fears losing his power as minister to Dumbledore. By using Umbridge to prevent the students of Hogwarts from learning how to duel, Fudge thinks he is preventing Dumbledore from raising an army against him.

Umbridge, wasting no time making her presence known, declares at the start-of-term feast, "Let us move forward, then, into a new era of openness, effectiveness and accountability, intent on preserving what ought to be preserved, perfecting what needs to be perfected, and pruning wherever we find practices that ought to be prohibited."[17] Umbridge singles out Harry for "spreading evil, nasty, attention-seeking stories."[18] (She even tortures him with a magical pen that concomitantly carves the words

Harry is forced to write in punishment—"I must not tell lies"—into the flesh on the back of his hand as he writes the words on paper.) Then, as High Inquisitor, and ultimately Headmaster, Umbridge institutes a strict authoritarian regime (devising edicts for any and every behavior, employing a truth serum to get information out of unwilling students, torturing students who do not obey, and organizing a squad of students to inform upon their fellow students in an attempt to crush any resistance). When Voldemort's Death Eaters eventually take over the ministry, Umbridge finds herself in her element among those who hold the same authoritarian views. In the final book, she chairs the Muggle-born Registration Commission and clearly relishes sending Muggle-borns to Azkaban (the magical world's horrific prison) and threatening them with the Dementor's Kiss (a foul creature that sucks the soul from its victim).

The sympathetic characters in the story are decidedly against Umbridge (and all those who exhibit such authoritarian tendencies). Harry refuses to submit to Umbridge's authority from the start, and his friends defy Umbridge repeatedly throughout the books. This is perhaps best celebrated in a scene depicted in the film *The Order of the Phoenix* in which the Weasley twins, Fred and George (Ron's twin older brothers) stage a disruption during the O.W.L.S. (what could be the wizarding equivalent of the S.A.T., another point of connection between Harry Potter and the Millennial experience, as will be discussed in the following chapter). Fred and George fly into the testing room, scattering test papers and ignite a fireworks display that not only includes a dragon that chases Umbridge out of the room but also destroys her entire wall of framed rules (the twins' rebellion in the book is, perhaps, a little less dramatic but no less effective).

In addition to fighting against Umbridge and the other authoritarian types in the books, Harry, Ron, and Hermione—indeed, all of the rest of the "good" characters in the books—display characteristics that are the opposite of the authoritarian predisposition. The good characters are open to new experiences, do not fear the unusual or the different, and, as discussed above, are extremely tolerant and accepting of everyone, regardless of their bloodlines or outward appearances. In this case, the lesson is quite clear for any immersed in the story: don't act like an authoritarian git.

Lesson 4: Violence and Torture Are Bad

... or perhaps in Slytherin
You'll make your real friends,
Those cunning folk use any means
To achieve their ends.[19]

Another frequent theme in the Harry Potter stories is that using violence freely and indiscriminately is a characteristic of bad people. The protagonists avoid violence, using it only when it is necessary—and sometimes, as with Harry, not even then—and abhor torture. As previously mentioned, in the "civilized" wizarding world there are three unforgivable curses: the Killing Curse (Avada Kedavra); the Cruciatus, or Torture Curse, which inflicts excruciating pain; and the *Imperius* curse, which allows the user to have absolute control over those upon whom it is cast. The antagonists use these curses without restraint and have no qualms about using them on children or others without the knowledge, skill, or even magic to fight back.

> Loud jeering, roars of laughter, and drunken yells were drifting towards them; then came a burst of strong green light, which illuminated the scene.
>
> A crowd of wizards, tightly packed and moving together with wands pointing straight upward, was marching slowly across the field. . . . High above them, floating along in midair, four struggling figures were being contorted into grotesque shapes. It was as though the masked wizards on the ground were puppeteers, and the [Muggles] above them were marionettes operated by invisible strings that rose from the wands into the air. Two of the figures were very small.[20]

As the evil Dark Lord, Voldemort is the quintessence of the notion that any means justify the ends, and his Death Eaters are more than happy to follow his lead. Indeed, in his search for immortality, when he was still the boy known as Tom Riddle and a student at Hogwarts, he thoroughly researched dark magic, carefully inquiring about Horcruxes.

> "You'd be hard-pushed to find a book at Hogwarts that'll give you details on Horcruxes, Tom, that's very Dark stuff, very Dark indeed," said

[Professor] Slughorn. . . . "A horcrux is the word used for an object in which a person has concealed part of their soul."

"I don't quite understand how that works, though, sir," said Riddle. His voice was carefully controlled, but Harry could sense his excitement.

"Well, you split your soul, you see," said Slughorn, "and hide part of it in an object outside of the body. Then, even if one's body is attacked or destroyed, one cannot die, for part of the soul remains earthbound and undamaged. . . . [T]he soul is supposed to remain intact and whole. Splitting it is an act of violation, it is against nature."[21]

Professor Slughorn explains that the only way to split one's soul is by committing a supreme act of evil: murder. Voldemort pushes him further, wanting to know about making more than one Horcrux, citing seven as a powerful number in magic, and wouldn't seven Horcruxes make a wizard that much more powerful. Slughorn is incredulous and replies that even thinking about killing one person is bad enough. But Voldemort has received the information he needs, and he creates the seven Horcruxes, allowing him to remain immortal and unbeatable as long as the Horcruxes exist.

Voldemort, even as a teenager, is clearly willing to kill—something considered so evil in Rowling's world that it "rips the soul apart"—in order to achieve his desires.[22] To see his convictions fulfilled is worth whatever it takes to do so, with no regard for anyone or anything. Voldemort's Death Eaters aren't always without reservations, but with full knowledge of how little their own lives might mean to him, they do his bidding without question. Draco is chosen to kill Dumbledore in the sixth book, *Harry Potter and the Half-Blood Prince*, and his efforts nearly kill two of his fellow students. In the final book, two Death Eaters, the Carrows, are in charge of discipline at Hogwarts. As Harry's friend Neville describes the situation to Harry, "They like punishment, the Carrows. . . . [T]hey make [Umbridge] look tame. . . . Amycus, the bloke, he teaches what used to be Defense Against the Dark Arts, except now it's just the Dark Arts. We're supposed to practice the Cruciatus Curse on people who've earned detentions. . . . They don't want to spill too much pure blood, so they'll torture us a bit if we're mouthy but they won't actually kill us."[23]

The best example of the aversion to violence and killing is found in Harry. He is horrified by the injured appearance of his friends who have stayed at Hogwarts in the final book and have been subjected to the careless cruelty Voldemort's followers have instituted there. Throughout all the books, Harry refuses to use the killing curse—even in the final showdown with Voldemort. As discussed earlier, his efforts at attempting the Cruciatus curse on Bellatrix Lestrange, who moments before had killed Sirius Black (a father figure to Harry and his only living connection to Harry's dead parents), is ineffective because even then, in his pain and rage, he is incapable of torturing someone because he doesn't truly mean it.

Harry is known for using disarmament against his attackers as opposed to harming them. In the final book, a plan is devised in order to prevent Death Eaters from attacking Harry when he leaves the Dursley's for the final time. Six wizards (including Ron and Hermione) drink a magical potion that makes them take on Harry's appearance; then those six and Harry take different routes. Harry, however, ruins the plan when he disarms a Death Eater during an attack. Remus Lupin admonishes Harry:

> "Harry, the time for Disarming is past! These people are trying to capture and kill you! At least stun if you aren't prepared to kill!"
>
> "We were hundreds of feet up! Stan's not himself, and if I stunned him and he'd fallen, he'd die the same as if I'd used Avada Kedavra! Expelliarmus saved me from Voldemort two years ago," Harry added defiantly.... "I won't blast people out of my way just because they're there," said Harry. "That's Voldemort's job."[24]

We suspect that the repetition of these themes about violence and torture—good people don't use these tactics, bad people do—will also have been internalized by fans of the series.

Lesson 5: Government Leaders Are Corrupt, Incompetent, and Fixated on Maintaining Power

Government in the Harry Potter series is portrayed in the Ministry of Magic, a secret cabinet within the British government that regulates the wizarding world, and a body many of the characters find inept and corrupt. "'Ministry o' Magic messin' things up as usual,' Hagrid muttered . . . 'They wanted Dumbledore fer Minister, o' course, but he'd never leave Hogwarts, so old Cornelius Fudge got the job. Bungler if ever there was one.'"[25] While the leaders of the Ministry of Magic are either bumbling, paranoid about losing power, incompetent, or corrupt, or some combination of the above, the problems with government are not necessarily portrayed as institutional in Harry Potter. For much of the series, the Ministry of Magic's executive office is held by Cornelius Fudge (note the name). Our first impression of Fudge is that he is self-important about his position but is, for the most part, friendly and sympathetic. It eventually becomes clear that his character is much more despicable than that. He is infatuated with tedious ministry regulations and takes bribes in the form of "donations" from families such as the Malfoys and then shows them favor over those who do not possess such bloodlines or money, such as the Weasleys. "You are blinded," Dumbledore tells Fudge, "by the love of the office you hold, Cornelius! You place too much importance, and you always have done, on the so-called purity of blood! You fail to recognize that it matters not what someone is born, but what they grow up to be!"[26]

Most despicably, though, instead of taking Harry's word about the return of Voldemort and preparing for it, he uses the *Daily Prophet* (a wizarding world newspaper) to discredit Harry and Dumbledore—who supports Harry and hopes to stop Voldemort. According to Professor Lupin, "Deep down, Fudge knows Dumbledore's much cleverer than he is, a much more powerful wizard, and in the early days of his Ministry he was forever asking Dumbledore for help and advice, [b]ut it seems that he's become fond of power now, and much more confident. He loves being Minister of Magic, and he's managed to convince himself that he's the clever one and Dumbledore's simply stirring up trouble for the sake of it. . . . [A]ccepting that Voldemort's back would mean trouble like the Ministry hasn't had to cope with for nearly fourteen years. . . . Fudge just can't bring himself to face it. It's so much more comfortable to convince himself that Dumbledore's lying to destabilize him."[27] Even the ministers who succeed Fudge are no better and are corrupted by Voldemort and his Death Eaters.[28]

The series' implicit critique of government, however, is limited to the individuals who are in charge. There is an accepted need for the regulations of the Ministry of Magic to keep the magical world hidden from the Muggle world and to maintain a responsible use of wizarding powers. Indeed, Harry's career goal is to work for the ministry as an Auror in what is, in effect, the ministry's security division.

We expect that the perspective on government the series offers—that individual politicians, not the institutions, are the problem—may have led to a set of attitudes about the real political world—in particular, a dim view of the George W. Bush administration—as well as a willingness to participate and a desire to remove the distrusted politicians and replace them with the opposition. At the same time that Millennials in the United States were reading the Harry Potter series, the Bush administration came under fire for, among other things, presenting a false case for war in Iraq, mishandling that war, ineptitude when it came to handling the damage caused by Hurricane Katrina, and the economic collapse of 2008. The Bush administration may have appeared to be bumbling, paranoid about losing power, incompetent, and corrupt. To readers of Harry Potter, we suspect that the Bush Administration looked exactly like the Ministry of Magic under Cornelius Fudge, with Vice President Dick Cheney as a convincing, if somewhat milder, Voldemort. Indeed, a bumper sticker surfaced near the end of Bush's term that read "Republicans for Voldemort." The Harry Potter series's lesson in how to remove such a corrupt and incompetent government, we hypothesize, might just have inspired fans to join the masses supporting Barack Obama's campaign of "hope and change."

Lesson 6: Be Skeptical, Not Cynical

Throughout the series Harry and his friends have to maintain a healthy level of skepticism. They are confronted repeatedly by things that are not what they first seem, governmental officials who are not to be trusted, and a media, particularly the wizarding world's sensationalist newspaper, the *Daily Prophet*, that has to be read with skepticism. With each new experience—from finding out about Hogwarts to discovering the true motives of Severus Snape—to each new character—good werewolves, witches, giants, and goblins—Harry realizes that nothing should be taken at face value.

In the third book, *Harry Potter and the Prisoner of Azkaban*, Harry learns a most important lesson about the benefits of being a skeptic. The title character is Sirius Black, the man suspected of informing Voldemort of Harry's parents whereabouts and, therefore, an accessory to their murder, despite being their friend. Sirius has escaped Azkaban, and everyone is convinced he is after Harry to finish the job. But after piecing together several clues and showing an ability to hear out the facts, Harry and his friends discover that Sirius is innocent and save him from an awful death.

The *Daily Prophet*'s vicious attacks on Harry and Professor Dumbledore, because they claim Voldemort has returned, make it clear that the media must be viewed with deep skepticism. Throughout the fourth novel, *Harry Potter and the Goblet of Fire*, Harry is hounded by one of the chief writers for the *Daily Prophet*, Rita Skeeter, as she covers the exciting wizarding tournament taking place at Hogwarts. When Harry first meets her she pulls him into a broom cupboard to do an interview:

> "You won't mind, Harry, if I use a Quick-Quotes Quill? It leaves me free to talk to you normally. . . . So, Harry . . . what made you decide to enter the Triwizard Tournament?"
>
> "Er—," said Harry again, but he was distracted by the quill. Even though he wasn't speaking, it was dashing across the parchment, and in its wake he could make out a fresh sentence:
>
> *An ugly scar, souvenir of a tragic past, disfigures the otherwise charming face of Harry Potter, who eyes—*
>
> "Ignore the quill, Harry," said Rita Skeeter firmly.[29]

Her embellishment continues, and it is easy to see how the *Daily Prophet* is not only a sensationalistic rag but also how it becomes a useful tool for Fudge to spread misinformation. After their encounters with Rita, Harry and his friends know enough to view anything written in the *Daily Prophet* with mistrust.

Their dealings with Fudge also help prepare Harry and his friends for Fudge's replacement in the final books. Rufus Scrimgeour has been head of Aurors when he replaces Fudge as minister, and although (unlike Fudge) he takes Voldemort seriously, his methods are not very effective—relying on warning pamphlets and bureaucracy. He arrests minor criminals or relatively innocent people and covers up major problems that Voldemort and the Death Eaters cause to put on a show that the Ministry is handling things effectively. He beseeches Harry to show the ministry some support and thereby boost his administration's public approval.

> "We ought to be working together."
> "I don't like your methods, Minister," said Harry. "Remember?" . . .
> [H]e raised his right fist and displayed to Scrimgeour the scars that still showed white on the back of it, spelling *I must not tell lies.* . . .
> "Maybe the Ministry should . . . [stop] wasting their time stripping down Deluminators or covering up breakouts from Azkaban. So this is what you've been doing Minister, shut up in your office, trying to break open a Snitch? People are dying—I was nearly one of them—Voldemort chased me across three counties, he killed Mad-Eye Moody, but there's been no word about any of that from the Ministry, has there? And still you expect us to cooperate with you!"[30]

Harry understands that despite being the minister in power and therefore technically capable of thwarting Voldemort's followers, Scrimgeour can't be trusted to do so. While this knowledge frustrates Harry, it does not stop him from acting.

While the protagonists maintain a healthy level of skepticism, they never become cynical. They try to get to the truth, to hold on to hope, to see the good in most everyone, and to trust those who have shown themselves trustworthy. The repetition of such lessons about skepticism versus cynicism throughout the series, we believe, should lead fans to exhibit the former over the latter.

While there are certainly more politically relevant lessons found in the Harry Potter series, such as advocating the need for collective action (this is not a story in the mold of typical US stories wherein the individual hero always wins the day), we focus on the six above because they recur throughout the series and often reinforce each other. Lessons that are repeated and reinforced are ones that fans will be most likely to learn. In the next chapter we discuss the psychological and social processes that explain how such political lessons found in entertainment media such as Harry Potter are internalized.

CHAPTER TWO

Learning the Lessons of the Wizarding World

Shedding some light on the politically relevant lessons of the Harry Potter series (Lumos Maxima, anyone?) is one thing; showing that the lessons had an effect on fans is quite another. After all, fans read the books and watched the films because they loved the story, not to learn political lessons. Indeed, one may be willing to accept that the Harry Potter series is not "just a story" and recognize that the series is clearly rich with political content but still argue that readers were simply enjoying a good story. And given that the series was read (or watched) for fun, the skeptic might ask why would anyone expect the politics of the series to have had an effect on fans? Well, dear skeptical reader (and, by the way, being a skeptic is a very good thing, so keep it up!), as it turns out, there are actually several bodies of research that give us good reasons to expect that reading and watching, even just for fun, *would* have an effect. After discussing these reasons, rooted in the scholarly theories and research findings of political socialization, generations, and media effects, the subsequent chapters discuss testing for actual evidence as to whether fans did indeed make the lessons of Harry Potter their own.

Passive and Incidental Learning

Scholars know that not all of what we take away from reading or watching is done actively or consciously; indeed, we learn a great deal about the world around us without even trying. Communication theorists differentiate between "active learning" and "passive learning."[1] Active learning is a conscious effort to learn material and concepts about something; in the process, the individual engages existing knowledge and beliefs to sort out the messages. Such active learning is not what we expect Harry Potter fans were doing when they read or watched. Passive learning, or incidental learning, on the other hand, occurs when learning is a byproduct of some other activity, such as reading for pleasure or watching movies for fun.[2] In the process of having fun, people are still exposed to politically relevant information, ideas, and lessons, and that exposure *can* lead to learning those perspectives. This is especially true when a person's cognitive defenses are down while enjoying entertainment—that is, they are not alert to, or ready to counter-argue, any political material—making them more susceptible to being influenced by the messages.

These notions of passive and incidental learning suggest that fans of Harry Potter may have internalized politically relevant lessons in a less-than-conscious way. In fact, we expect the likelihood that the Harry Potter series affected fan's politics may have been enhanced because the acquisition of the political perspectives that exist in the series was a by-product of reading it for fun. Because this is a case of passive learning, the Harry Potter series is likely to have had an effect on fans even if those fans already had the political values and information to counter-argue the political lessons it contained (which for many fans was not likely since they were so young when they started to read the series).

While passive learning is often characterized as temporary, the repetition of the lessons as fans read through all seven of the books (often more than once) and watched the eight movies (often more than once), in addition to the overlapping and reinforcing nature of the lessons themselves, would likely go a long way to making these lessons more permanent. The repeated exposure to the lessons of Harry Potter suggests that cultivation theory might apply here, as well. Cultivation theory hypothesizes that repeated exposure to a media source leads audiences to internalize the perspectives of that source and to see the world as similar to the world portrayed in that media. Evidence to support cultivation theory has been found in research that shows that people who watch a lot of television see the world as it is presented on television.[3] The desire of fans to repeatedly visit and immerse themselves in the world of the boy wizard—as evidenced by the Quidditch teams, the fan sites, and the costumed throngs forming midnight lines outside bookshops and movie theaters—makes us suspect that a cultivation effect may have occurred among Harry Potter fans so that the internalization of the perspectives of the series happened in a manner that had a more lasting effect on the politics of Millennials.

Political Socialization

Despite the evidence behind passive and incidental learning effects, the notion that a book and film series about a boy wizard (or any other entertainment media, for that matter) may have helped form political views is undoubtedly greeted with continued skepticism by many readers. Either you dismiss the notion entirely or, if you think there may be a bit of truth to it, you believe that the entertainment media would not affect *you*. Such skeptical reactions may originate from an inaccurate assumption about how people develop their political selves.[4] Most of us like to think we arrived at our perspectives of the political world through a rational, fact-based process, but, as the overwhelming evidence in different fields of study shows, we are fooling ourselves to believe so. Additionally, it is not true that we are born with all of our political perspectives programmed in our genes. Instead, most of how we see the political world is developed through an interactive learning process that scholars have labeled "political socialization."

Political socialization theory posits that we acquire our politically relevant values and perspectives from our culture. We don't just do so through osmosis; instead, there are "agents" of socialization that transmit the cultural values, information, and political perspectives of a society to each new generation. Put another way, we learn how to act and what to value in our society from *people*—such as our families and our friends or members of our community—and *institutions*—such as schools, religious institutions, and the media (television, video games, movies, and books). The learning occurs largely through our observations of the behavior of these agents of socialization, who "can be as intimate and close as members of the family, *or as remote as heroes read about or viewed*."[5]

The importance of each agent to an individual's political socialization depends on the level of attachment or connection to the agent and the level of homogeneity among socializing agents—that is, whether those agents conform to the perspectives shared by other agents or represent different sets of values. Parents are considered the most important agents

for values learned early in life because of the emotional bond that typi-
cally exists between parent and child. Outside of family, you may have
connected with a friend or teacher who had a powerful effect on how you
see the world. Recent research in political socialization has reinforced
earlier findings of the importance of various agents of socialization, including parental influence on partisanship, presidential vote choice, racial
attitudes, school prayer, and attitudes regarding business versus labor;[6]
the influence of schools and communities on civic engagement, political
participation, and political tolerance;[7] and, the effect of news and entertainment media, including reading, on social capital and civic activity.[8] In
figure 2.1 we list the major political socializing agents and their level of
influence, drawn from a set of in-depth interviews with University of Vermont students.[9] For most respondents, parents were the dominant influence (reflecting the findings of the research on political socialization), but
books and films were found to have had a strong or moderate influence
on the political views of over one-third of those interviewed (for 40%,
films had a strong or moderate influence; for 36%, books).

Reinforcing Effects

Agents of socialization that share the same perspectives tend to reinforce
each other. So, for example, if your friends come from families that share
the same values as your parents, your friends will reinforce the values you
acquired from your parents. If your parents determine the media you are
exposed to, then the books, films and television you watch will likely reinforce your parents' values. So while some parents may have encouraged
their children to read the Harry Potter series because of its values (though
most probably encouraged the series simply because it got their child to
read), others, such as conservative Christians, may have tried to dissuade
their children from reading the series because of its positive portrayal of
magic, witches, and wizards, which clashed with their values.[10] When we
asked Millennials whether their parents had a role in them reading the
books, we found that 33 percent of those who read the books said that
their parents encouraged them to read the books (or read them with or to
them).

That an agent of socialization was found to have reinforced the effect

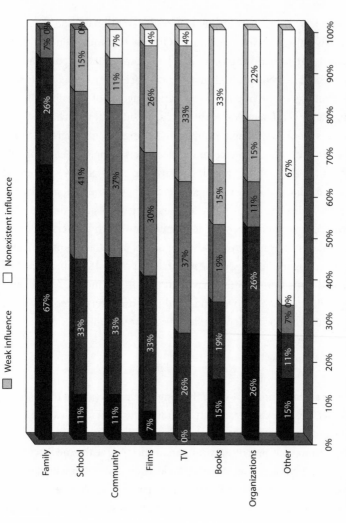

Figure 2.1. Influence of agents of political socialization. From in-depth interviews of University of Vermont students, conducted by the students of POLS237, Film, TV and Public Opinion, fall semester 2006, n = 27 (methodology available upon request).

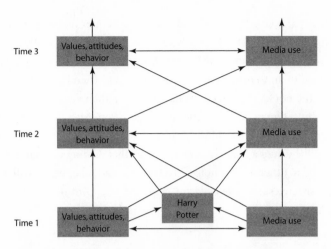

Figure 2.2. Reinforcing spirals of influence and the role of Harry Potter. Adapted from Slater, "Reinforcing Spirals."

of other agents is sometimes interpreted to mean that the reinforcing agents are not important. But the reinforcement of values and perspectives is important in its own right. Reinforcement strengthens the values and perspectives learned. It reduces the likelihood that those values will change later in life. And it increases the power of those values and perspectives to shape other values and perspectives through selective exposure to other agents (friends, work associates, *and* media choices) and the interpretation of other political messages. Indeed, some scholars argue that reinforcing media effects operate through "spirals of influence" to exert powerful effects on individuals.[11] Media choices and receptiveness to media messages are determined in part by existing attitudes (shaped by agents of political socialization, including other media), which then affect future media choices and the influence of those choices (see fig. 2.2).

Since some fans of Harry Potter may have taken up the series at the urging of other agents of socialization—parents, siblings, friends, school-teachers—who at some level may have liked the books for the values they taught, the influence of Harry Potter may have been to reinforce the values learned from those other agents of socialization. In those cases, the reinforcing effect should not be trivialized. It may be that the Harry Potter series strengthened the perspectives learned from the fans' parents. It may be that it enabled them to disregard or counter messages that went against the lessons of the Harry Potter series, say, for example, the attitude toward torture promoted by the television series *24*.[12] It may be that the series led them to develop closer connections to friends who shared the values the books reinforced, values that were then again reinforced by the friends. It may be that becoming a Harry Potter fan opened the door to a community of like-minded individuals whose very existence could bolster the values a fan held. And it may be that reading the Harry Potter series led to other media choices, led them to read other books with similar perspectives, say *The Golden Compass* or the Lord of the Rings that may have even further reinforced their perspectives.

Independent Effects

Given the immense popularity and scope of exposure to the Harry Potter series, however, it is highly likely that for many fans, the world of the boy wizard offered some perspectives that were either absent or not emphasized by the other agents in their socialization (64% of Millennials we surveyed said their parents *did not* play a role in their decision to read the Harry Potter books, 3% said their parents discouraged them from reading the books). In our conversations with Millennials, we found a variety of ways in which fans were introduced to the series. When asked when and where they came in contact with the series, one fan responded: "I think it was second grade, I can't exactly remember how I heard about HP. I think, well the earliest I can remember was the news, a news show done about the opening of the second book and how huge it was and everyone was buying it. So I was like, what is this book? And so I had my mom go out and get it and I started reading it. Just hooked right away."[13] Another said, "I used to always sleep over at my friend Elizabeth's house and every night her Mom would always read the books to her, and well her brother and sister. And, I mean I wasn't always there but that was my first exposure to the books. And I think that in the third grade there was just that buzz about the books and our library had this big mural of like, HP kind of things. And I remember the person who did it was this kid's, Jack Potter's[,] Mom, and that was funny. I just remember his name. Yeah. I was in third grade when the third book came out. But that was when I first started to be more aware of it. And there was this hallway of our school that we called Diagon Alley, I don't know why. It was actually a really creepy hallway."[14] Others told us that they got into Harry Potter in a variety of other ways, including at camp when a bunkmate's mother sent a copy, when a relative sent it as a Christmas present, when a teacher read it in second grade, and when a librarian read snippets of one the books at school.

A child may have become a fan of Harry Potter because the world of the boy wizard offered an escape from the difficulties of the real world of the preteen years or adolescence, an escape where they could find characters their age struggling with the same problems. Then, after becoming a fan, that child may have connected with other children who were also fans, ultimately joining the broader Harry Potter fan community. Parents may have promoted the series to their children not because of the values in the books but because they learned from other parents that the books were great at encouraging reading.

Political socialization agents with different sets of values offer alternative perspectives that can affect a person's political views. Such influence may occur if, say, you watch a television show that demonstrates a different attitude from those extant in your environment. Indeed, for individuals growing up in politically homogeneous communities, the media—books, television, movies, comic books—may be the *only* set of agents to offer alternative perspectives. As teens, my brother and I secretly watched *Saturday Night Live* (*SNL*) and *Monty Python's Flying Circus*. We had to watch the programs surreptitiously because our parents had banned the shows for their irreverent attitude, or as our mother put it about *SNL*, "because they made fun of the president." *SNL* and *Monty Python* were the only political socialization agents I was exposed to that evinced irreverence, and, as a result, these shows played a formative role in my generally irreverent disposition and subsequent preference for other media outlets that mirror that attitude, such as *South Park* and *The Daily Show*. Similarly, the Harry Potter series undoubtedly introduced its fans to perspectives that were not part of their socialization environment. It may be that the series provided a window onto a much more diverse world than the one in which they lived, along with the lessons promoting respect and tolerance of those who are different. It may also be that Harry Potter offered an alternative conception of authority or perspectives on torture and deadly violence that were not learned from other socialization agents.

Both the reinforcing effect of political socialization agents with similar perspectives and the independent effect of agents with different values are important to one's political socialization—one strengthens values and builds confidence in political perspectives; the other explains how agents can have a unique, independent effect on political views and ensures that we do not simply become political clones of our parents (or any other single socializing agents). We suspect that the Harry Potter series, which was such an important part of the early lives of so many Millennials, was certainly an important agent in their political socialization. It may have functioned to reinforce the values of other socialization agents for some, but, given the immense popularity and reach of the story of the boy wizard, it likely had an independent effect on many more.

Adolescence and the Formative Years

There is another dimension of political socialization that offers more reasons to expect that the Harry Potter series had an effect on the politics of Millennials and that is the idea that certain age periods in people's lives are more important than others in the formation of political views. During the process of political socialization, what is learned depends on the developmental stage of the individual. Early learning involves largely emotional attachments and the development of diffuse support; it is a time when parents play an important role.[15] Later in the process, during adolescence, individuals develop abilities to think in more abstract terms and are thus more capable of dealing with the concepts involved in politics and government. Finally, by around the age of seventeen (plus or minus a few years), individuals begin to form their political views, questioning and reflecting on perspectives of previous generations, testing those perspectives against their own experiences.[16] It is during the periods of adolescence and the formative years that the political and social environment has its biggest impact on the values and outlooks that form the basis of a person's politics. During adolescence, individuals are being exposed to politically relevant messages that they can comprehend for the first time, and since they comprehend this material for the first time, they are less likely to have already existing beliefs that could filter out or counter-argue those messages. In essence, during a person's adolescence and formative years of political socialization, they are more vulnerable to political influence because they don't have the preexisting attitudes that are the basis for selective exposure, perception, and retention of politically relevant messages. Put another way, strongly held beliefs at this stage of political development are likely absent: adolescents are not likely to be selecting media based on political values; they are more open to perceiving a wide variety of politically relevant messages and will thus be more likely to retain the memories of the perspectives learned. It was during these adolescent years that most Millennial fans developed a love for the Harry Potter series, a passionate interest that carried through into their formative years.

The importance of adolescence and the formative years of political socialization are recognized by the theories and research regarding generations. Age cohorts are made into generations during their formative years by the historical circumstances they find themselves in. As they awaken to politics, the times (politics, economic conditions, state of the world, technological developments, and cultural events) leave a permanent and unique imprint on the generation, shaping the way its members see and interact with the world.[17] For the Millennial Generation, the Harry Potter series did not just affect individual fans but, given its immense popularity, played a role in shaping the political socialization of a generation.

Identification and Modeling

In addition, the timing of the Harry Potter series couldn't have been better for Millennials to identify with the story's protagonists, thus enhancing the potential impact of the series. Millennials didn't just read the Harry Potter books and watch the movies, they actually *grew up along with the characters of the series*; they aged along with Harry, Hermione, and Ron, and in doing so they confronted in their own lives many of the same issues confronting the characters. Millennials didn't just read the stories, but read them multiple times ("countless" times, as some put it), dressed up as the characters, joined fan groups, created their own Harry Potter stories, art, and music. Many even expected to receive a letter inviting them to attend Hogwarts when they turned eleven (as I heard from more than a few students who were disappointed that the anticipated letter never showed up). Even if they didn't think they actually were going to Hogwarts, many took the Hogwarts House personality test, which, for one fan, created an even deeper connection to the series: "I also felt like it was a cool way to connect, to feel like you're part of the world too, like oh, where would I be? You know and I think about how often, and especially, I'm sure you feel the same way too, but it being the last thing I did before I fell asleep, like it took my mind to crazy places and I always wanted to be there, and I imagined myself being there. It was definitely cooler to know, or guess where I might have been sorted."[18] Among those we interviewed were Gryffindors, Ravenclaws, Hufflepuffs, and even Slytherins (when we took the test, Gierzynski was sorted into Gryffindor and Eddy into Ravenclaw).

Such immersion means that much of the generation identified with the characters to a degree that the characters became models for learning.[19] Immersion leads to what has been called "transportation," which

> is presumed to affect not only the perceived entertainment value of the media, but also the cognitive and emotional responses of the viewer. Individuals who are transported are more likely to process the messages of the narrative via peripheral route processing, with fewer negative cognitive responses and greater affective response. . . .
>
> As a reader or viewer of a narrative becomes more immersed in its events, the narrative world, its inhabitants, and its situations begin to feel more real, and the consumer responds both emotionally and cognitively as if they were. Thus we treat the things that happen within it much as we do stimuli within the real world itself. Over time we may eventually begin to see the real world through the filter of the media-created worlds into which we feel most transported, rather than the other way around.[20]

The power of fictional narratives to engender identification with the characters of a story has even been demonstrated using readings from the Harry Potter series in an experimental study—the experimental group that read selections from Harry Potter psychologically became wizards (those who read selections from the *Twilight* series became vampires).[21] As Millennial adolescents identified with the characters and became immersed in the Harry Potter series during their formative years, there is good reason to expect that fans adopted many of their values.[22]

One final note on Harry Potter as an agent of political socialization for Millennials: the Potter phenomenon was more than just a set of books and movies that Millennials got hooked on; it also created an active and visible community of fans. Being part of a community strengthens the learning of values shared by that community. Indeed, social relationships have the "most important impact . . . on motivational processes of social learning theory."[23] If you were a Millennial growing up obsessed with Harry Potter, it should have been abundantly clear that you were not alone, that your passion was shared by a very large community of fans. Given its popularity, the odds were pretty good that there were children your age in school with whom you could talk about the series. There were Internet-based fan communities where you could interact with other fans. And the news media covered the immensely popular phenomenon every time there was a new book or movie released. All of this should have worked to reinforce or strengthen the impact the lessons of series had on its fans.

The Harry Potter phenomenon happened in a way that made it an important agent of political socialization for Millennials. The series hit the Millennial Generation in their politically vulnerable years and engendered deep and widespread interest at an age when selective exposure and the ability to counter-argue are minimal. Its popularity led to the development of a Harry Potter fan community that strengthened the impact of the series and heightened the effect of the politically relevant lessons from the wizarding world.

Harry Potter and the Millennial Generation

While the story of the boy who lived found fans in several generations, the Harry Potter series was by far the most popular for those who were near the age of the characters (about eleven) when the first book arrived on the scene in 1997—the members of the Millennial generation. (The first books were actually targeted for a young adult reading level—Millennials when they were in their preteen years—and the books increased in sophistication as the characters and their Millennial generation fans aged.) Harry Potter was an important ingredient in the making of the Millennial generation. Since Harry Potter was a Millennial generation phenomenon, we have focused our research on the series's effects on the members of that generation who became fans. When historians examine the historical, cultural, and political factors that shaped the character of the Millennials they will need to recognize the role played by the Harry Potter phenomenon or their portrait of the generation will be incomplete. Leaving Harry Potter out of the history of Millennials would be like leaving *Star Wars* out of the story of Generation X, or the Beatles out of the history of Boomers, or *Casablanca* out of the story of the GI Generation.

Generations

In a classic essay, Karl Mannheim argued that a generation is formed when the character of the political and social environment of a time leaves a permanent imprint on the political psyche of the segment of the population who are in their formative years of political socialization.[24] The result is a group delineated by age but defined by history, a generation sharing a common set of political perspectives that sets them apart from other age cohorts. Mannheim also argued that generational units may form within generations.

The generational unit represents a much more concrete bond than the actual generation as such. "Youth experiencing the same concrete historical problems may be said to be part of the same actual generation; while those groups within the same actual generation which work up the material of their common experiences in different specific ways, constitute separate generation units."[25] While the Harry Potter series constituted a generation-wide phenomenon, it is also possible that being a fan of the boy wizard resulted in the development of a generational unit within the Millennial Generation.

A few things about the idea of generations are important to note. First, the manner of conceptualizing generations used here is different from demographers' perspective on generations. Demographers base generations on trends in birth rates (hence the "baby boom" generation). This view of generations is of little use to those who wish to understand the character of a generation beyond its size; it plays down the importance of historical and cultural circumstances, as well as the socialization process, which are very important for developing an understanding of the politics of a generation. Second, there is a methodological difficulty in empirically defining a generation.[26] The methodological issue makes it statistically impossible to parse separate age, time, and generational effects, and as a consequence it is difficult to offer definitive evidence of the existence of generations. Yet that methodological problem has not impeded the development of strong theoretical arguments (see Mannheim's essay) for, or the amassing of evidence about, the unique character of different age cohorts to identify them as generations. Works by Neil Howe and William Strauss and by Moreley Winograd and Michael D. Hais have focused on the Millennials and offer the conceptualization of generations we utilize here.[27] Howe and Strauss delineate the current generations as follows:

- G.I. Generation, born 1901–1924;
- Silent Generation, born 1925–1942;
- Baby Boom Generation, born 1943–1960;
- Generation X, born 1961–1981;
- Millennial Generation, born 1982–2002.[28]

The Millennial Generation

The oldest Millennials were sixteen years of age when *Harry Potter and the Sorcerer's Stone* was published in 1997. As for the age of the youngest Millennials when the first book came out, that depends on when the generation ends. Writing before the last of Millennials were born, Howe and Strauss could not be confident of the end date for that generation. We suspect that those born after 1992 may be of a different generation or at least a different "wave" of the generation. (Similarly, Howe and Strauss described Gen X as having two separate waves, the "Atari Wave" and the "Nintendo Wave.") Those who were born after 1992 were too young to vote in the 2008 presidential election or to participate fully in that movement of hope and change (two-thirds of eighteen-to-twenty-nine-year-olds voted for Obama[29]). The problems faced by the world during this newer cohort's formative years seem intractable. The acceleration of technology and near total assimilation to social media seems to have altered radically the nature of their relationship with the world of information. For them, the Harry Potter series was probably experienced first on the big screen rather than in print. Exactly where you put the end point of the Millennial Generation is not important to settle here; what is important is to note that the influence of the Harry Potter series was undoubtedly greatest for those Millennials born between 1982 and 1992. That is the group that was between the ages of six and sixteen when the *Sorcerer's Stone* first appeared; they were between the ages of eight and eighteen when the popularity of the series really took off with the publication of *Harry Potter and the Chamber of Secrets* and *Harry Potter and the Prisoner of Azkaban* in 1999.

Obviously, the Harry Potter series was not the only ingredient that shaped Millennials' perspectives. Early in 2008 (prior to our interest regarding the effect of Harry Potter), I asked a group of students what they thought defined their generation. That question turned into a research project in which the students identified the most important historical and social developments that shaped the psyche of their generation (they were all Millennials). They identified the school shootings in Columbine, Colorado; the Monica Lewinsky scandal; cell phones; the 2000 presidential election; the development of the Internet; September 11, 2001; the Bush presidency; reality TV; wars in Afghanistan and Iraq; hip-hop culture; Hurricane Katrina; global warming, Facebook, YouTube, the move toward same-sex marriage, *and* Harry Potter.[30] Add the great recession of 2008 and the election of Barack Obama and you have a list that many scholars who write about the generation would not dispute.[31] As for the role Harry Potter played, the students wrote that the series

> got kids to read massive books in a matter of a few days; made literature a strong form of entertainment again. Harry Potter was more than a series of seven award-winning novels. Harry Potter was one of the great cultural events of our generation's time. Harry Potter helped raise the children of our generation by instilling in them some of the basic moral conceptions of right and wrong. In the series there is a very clear "good side," epitomized by Harry Potter, which embodies the basic

qualities of love, loyalty, courage, and forgiveness. Juxtaposed is a very clear "bad side," epitomized by He-Who-Must-Not-Be-Named, which embodies all of the negative qualities of deceitfulness, vengeance, and killing. . . . The Harry Potter series is very pronounced in the views that it expresses; views that were instilled in our generation through this popular series of books.[32]

Exposure to the Harry Potter series was so widespread for such an extended period of time (from the release of the first book in 1997 to the release of the last movie in 2011) that it engaged a large proportion of Millennials very deeply. The breadth and depth of the popularity of the Harry Potter phenomenon during the adolescent and formative years of the Millennial Generation meant that there was a high level of exposure to the lessons of Harry Potter at a critical time for their generation. Clearly, the story of the boy who lived has a prominent place among the important factors that shaped the Millennial Generation both broadly speaking and with regard to that unit of Millennials who became fans of the series.

Reading

The Harry Potter series entered popular culture at a time when reading for pleasure was in decline in the United States. Some have speculated that the series stemmed that decline among the youth to whom it so appealed. According to a study produced by the National Endowment for the Arts in 2007, only 57 percent of adults read any books for pleasure, and "Americans in almost every demographic group were reading fiction, poetry, and drama—and books in general—at significantly lower rates than 10 or 20 years earlier."[33] Furthermore, when young Americans read, they often use other media concurrently, weakening comprehension and the effects of reading.[34]

The downward trend in reading is *not* a good thing for society or democracy. Reading for pleasure is associated with higher grades, as well as with higher reading-comprehension and writing scores.[35] With reading comes an enhanced cognitive capacity that allows for a greater ability to deal with complexity.[36] Because of its role in enhancing cognitive capacity, those who read may also be *less* likely to develop a predisposition toward authoritarianism (the antidemocratic predisposition that leads to intolerance and racial and ethnic hatred).[37] Those who read are more engaged civically; they are more likely to volunteer, to play a role in civic and cultural life, and to vote.[38] As summed up by the chairman of the National Endowment for the Arts (NEA), Dana Gioia, in the introduction to the agency's 2007 review of all the research and data on reading in the United States: "*To Read or Not To Read* confirms—without any serious qualification—the central importance of reading for a prosperous, free society. The data here demonstrate that reading is an irreplaceable activity in developing productive and active adults as well as healthy communities. Whatever the benefits of newer electronic media, they provide no measurable substitute for the intellectual and personal development initiated and sustained by frequent reading."[39]

The impact Harry Potter had on the reading habits of members of the Millennial Generation is the final point that leads us to expect the Harry Potter series has had an effect on them. By all popular accounts the story of the boy who lived appeared to have enticed many children to read books for fun, many of whom may not otherwise have taken up the habit. There are hints that the series may have slowed and even reversed the downward trend in reading. Take book sales, for instance: "In 2000, more than 1.6 billion consumer books were purchased in the U.S.—a record high. One possible reason for the spike in unit sales is the Harry Potter series: J. K. Rowling's fourth book was released in hardback in January 2000, and a paperback version of the second book became available in August of that year."[40] Media use studies by the Kaiser Family Foundation and the U.S. Department of Education conducted during the Harry Potter era found improvement in time spent reading among the age group that were the most likely to become fans. Unlike other age groups, nine-year-olds in the late 1990s and early 2000s showed no declines in voluntary reading and an increase in reading scores.[41] Media-use patterns in 2003–2004 showed that 40 percent of eight-to-ten-year-olds were found to have read thirty minutes or more the previous day as compared to 27 percent of eleven-to-fourteen-year-olds.[42] While these data are suggestive, they cannot prove that the arrival of the Harry Potter series caused more Millennials to read, but we have one more piece of data from our survey to add to the argument (methods and full results of the survey are discussed in the next chapter). When we asked respondents directly about the role that the Harry Potter series played in their reading habits, fully 17 percent of our sample said, "I was not much of a reader until I read the Harry Potter *series*, but after reading Harry Potter, I began to read more books." In-depth interviews reinforced these findings.[43] "It took a text like Harry Potter to really intrigue me to enjoy reading and I don't think I ever enjoyed reading as much as I did reading those books so that got me to bypass that comprehension barrier. Since then, I've never had that problem again—thank you JKR!"[44] "[I] absolutely started reading, 100 percent because of Harry Potter. I was in fifth grade and the only time I really enjoyed reading, actually I don't even know, the book *Holes*, before that. No other big series, I mean like, when I was younger the Berenstain Bears and things like that. But not in any real way, not real books with chapters, and not in the way that I read Harry Potter and the way they got me to search out books I enjoyed. So it absolutely got me to read more, I mean I tell people this all the time, Harry Potter one hundred percent got me into reading."[45]

Given the low and declining levels of reading for pleasure in the United States, the effect of the Harry Potter series on Millennials' reading habits has been huge. The evidence from our research, along with the data on reading, book sales, and the general talk about the series, convinces us that many more Millennials are readers *because* of the Harry Potter books.[46] That is a finding of great consequence. It means that the tale of the boy wizard likely shaped politically relevant views not just through the lessons that it offered but also by the fact that it made readers out of many Millennials who otherwise might not have picked up the habit of reading for pleasure. So, for example, we hypothesize that the Harry Potter series reduced the proportion of Millennials with the authoritarian predisposition not simply due to its portrayal of authoritarian types in the series (see chap. 1) but also indirectly by getting Millennials to read, which in turn enhanced their cognitive skills and subsequently their ability to deal with complexity and difference (in addition to the story's lessons in acceptance of differences, as also discussed in chap. 1).

Hypotheses

Bringing together the political content of the Harry Potter stories (detailed in the previous chapter) with the expectations engendered by political socialization theory, learning theory, and the effects of reading, we arrived at the following set of hypotheses regarding the political impact of the series on the Millennial Generation.

- Hypothesis 1: Fans of Harry Potter will exhibit a greater acceptance than nonfans of diversity and differences (derived from Lesson 1 in chap. 1).
- Hypothesis 2: Fans of Harry Potter will exhibit greater levels of political tolerance than do nonfans (Lesson 2).
- Hypothesis 3: Fans of Harry Potter will value equality more than nonfans (Lesson 2).
- Hypothesis 4: Fans of Harry Potter will be less likely than nonfans to exhibit the authoritarian predisposition (Lesson 3).
- Hypothesis 5: Fans of Harry Potter will be less supportive of the use of deadly force than nonfans (Lesson 4).
- Hypothesis 6: Fans of Harry Potter will be less likely than nonfans to support the use of torture (Lesson 4).
- Hypothesis 7: Fans of Harry Potter will have a more negative view of the Bush administration than do nonfans (Lesson 5).
- Hypothesis 8: Fans of Harry Potter will participate in politics at a higher rate than nonfans (Lesson 5).
- Hypothesis 9: Fans of Harry Potter will have supported Barack Obama for president at a higher rate than will nonfans (Lesson 5).
- Hypothesis 10: Fans of Harry Potter will evince a greater level of skepticism and a lower level of cynicism than nonfans (Lesson 6).

In the next two chapters we test these hypotheses using survey data and the words of Millennials themselves.

CHAPTER THREE

Do the Politics of Harry Potter Fans Reflect Those of the Wizarding World?

Having shed light on the politically relevant content of the Harry Potter series and having provided solid reasons why it would have contributed to the political development of Millennials, we now turn to empirical evidence. This chapter and chapter 4 offer an analysis of survey results and interviews that supports our hypotheses regarding the Potter effect among Millennials. While there are several methodological issues to weigh in assessing the results of such a study, the findings ultimately do lend support to the theoretical arguments of the previous chapter, which suggests that the series did play a role in the development of the political perspectives of the Millennial Generation.

How We Carried Out Our Study

To look for evidence for the Harry Potter effect, we developed and implemented a survey of college-aged Millennials in 2009. We also collected qualitative data via interviews and essays from 2009 to 2011 to capture the thoughts of Millennials themselves about the Harry Potter effect.

The survey we ran was an anonymous, pencil-and-paper survey designed as part of class project in the undergraduate research seminar Film, TV and Public Opinion at the University of Vermont.[1] Students in classrooms at the University of Vermont took the first wave of the survey in the spring semester of 2009 while colleagues at Mississippi State University and the University of Mississippi (Ole Miss) ran the surveys in classes at their schools.[2] Given the positive results of the first wave of the survey, we ran another wave of the survey in the fall 2009 semester, reaching classes at Adirondack Community College in upstate New York, California Polytechnic State University, Iowa State University, and Pacific Lutheran University.[3] The total sample from this diverse set of institutions was 1,141. The sample was not a random sample; however, the diversity of schools in which the survey was run and the very high response rate afforded by these captive samples (less than 1% of surveys were spoiled) make us confident that we obtained a diverse sample of college Millennials in the United States, an adequate sample to test our hypotheses. More information on the sample and methods can be found in appendix A.

In the survey we asked questions designed to measure exposure to Harry Potter along with questions that measured the perspectives we believe were affected by exposure to the lessons of the story of the boy who lived (see the hypotheses at the end of chap. 2). The full survey in the form in which it was administered can be found in appendix B.

Measuring Levels of Harry Potter Fandom

We devised several ways to measure exposure to the lessons of Harry Potter among respondents. We asked how many of the Harry Potter books respondents had read and how many of the movies they had seen. Testifying to the popularity of the series among Millennials, 35 percent of respondents had read all the books while a total of two-thirds had read at least some of the books; 45 percent had seen all the movies and 86 percent had seen at least some of the movies (see figs. 3.1 and 3.2). It is important to note that some fans of the books were not fans of the movies. Indeed, 24 percent who read all of the books did not see all of the movies. Thus the questions about reading the books and watching the movies probably measure slightly different fan types. The most avid fans, we believed, would be the ones who read all of the books at least once (if not repeatedly).

We also asked respondents to place themselves on a five-point fan scale, one end of which represented fans who were very much into the Harry Potter series and the other, those who hadn't read or seen any of the series or, if they did, hated it. Twenty-nine percent picked the highest level of fandom, and a total of half the respondents considered themselves fans in the top two categories of the scale (see fig. 3.3). Even though the survey was anonymous, the fact that so many Millennials identified themselves as fans is astounding given the potential for being labeled a geek

How many Harry Potter books have you read?

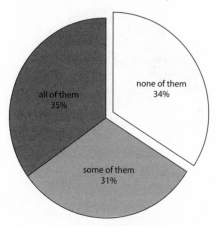

Figure 3.1. Harry Potter books read (margin of error at 95% confidence level ±2.9%).

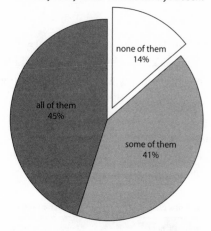

Figure 3.2. Harry Potter movies seen.

(these were college students after all). The fear of being ridiculed for being into Harry Potter was evident even in the all-Harry-Potter-fan seminar that first took up this project; it took a while for students to feel comfortable talking about how into the series they were despite the fact they were

Harry Potter fan scale

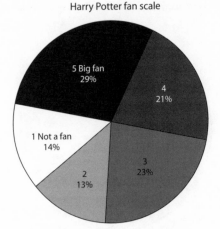

Figure 3.3. Fan scale (5 represents respondents who were "very much into Harry Potter"; 1 represents respondents who were people who haven't read or seen any of the series or, if they have, hated it).

in a room full of fellow fans. Given this stigma, it says a lot that a large segment of our sample picked the highest level of fandom.

Finally, we asked respondents who had read the books or seen the movies a series of increasingly difficult Harry Potter trivia questions, some of which, at the time of the survey, could only have been answered by reading the books. Fourteen percent got all of the trivia questions correct; another 10 percent answered four of the five questions correctly (test your knowledge with these questions).

Harry Potter Trivia Questions Designed to Measure Immersion in the Series

1. Who is the Half Blood Prince?				
a. Severus Snape	b. Harry Potter	c. Voldemort	d. Draco Malfoy	e. I don't know
2. Who is Peeves?				
a. Professor of Muggle Studies	b. Harry's secret crush	c. A troublesome poltergeist at Hogwarts	d. Dumbledore's Phoenix	e. I don't know

3. What is Ron's position in Quidditch?				
a. Seeker	b. Keeper	c. Chaser	d. Beater	e. I don't know
4. Which of the magical spells wards off Dementor attacks?				
a. Alohomora	b. Avada Kedavra	c. Expecto Patronum	d. Stupefy	e. I don't know
5. The vanishing cabinet connects Hogwarts to				
a. Malfoy's Mansion	b. The Shrieking Shack	c. The Hog's Head	d. Borgin & Burke's	e. I don't know

Answers are located at the end of appendix A.

The words of Millennials themselves on the effect of the Harry Potter series come from a series of personal interviews conducted by research seminar students and from reflective personal history essays assigned to students in other classes (see appendix A for more information on these studies).

Did Harry Potter Fans Internalize the Lessons of the Series?

In order to test for the effect of the lessons of the story of the boy wizard, we asked respondents questions designed to measure their perspectives relevant to those lessons and then compared the responses of Potter fans and nonfans. The idea was to see whether among Millennials Harry Potter fans differed from nonfans on the political perspectives that were at the heart of the lessons of the series.

Lesson 1: Diversity and Acceptance; or, Don't Judge People (or Creatures) by Their Appearance or Blood

To test whether the role models of acceptance of diversity offered by the Harry and his friends were mirrored in the fans of the series we asked respondents how they felt about several groups who have been subject to discrimination in the United States—Muslims, African Americans, undocumented immigrants, and homosexuals. Specifically, we did this by asking them to rate their feelings on a five point "feeling thermometer" from a score of 0 for "0°, very cold or unfavorable feeling" to a score of 4 for "100°, very warm or favorable feeling." We then added up each person's total of feeling scores toward all the groups and compared the average feeling score total of Harry Potter fans and nonfans (range of actual scores was between 4 and 16). The results are shown in figure 3.4. Those who read all of the books, as compared to the rest of the sample, evinced statistically significant warmer feelings toward the different groups we asked about (averaging a 14.0 total on the additive score of feeling thermometer questions as compared to a 12.9 average for nonfans). This finding suggests a greater acceptance of differences on the part of Harry Potter fans.[4] This difference in feelings between fans and nonfans held true regardless of how we measured Potter fandom—Millennials' self-placement on the fan scale and the number of trivia questions they got correct both were positively correlated with their overall feelings toward these diverse groups.[5] Millennials who saw all the movies also had a higher average feeling score than those who did not.[6]

Lesson 2: Political Tolerance and Equality; or, Everyone Has the Same Rights to Dignity and Freedom

To determine whether Harry Potter fans evinced tolerant attitudes akin to those of Harry and his friends, we compared fans and nonfans on their scores from questions designed to measure political tolerance.[7] The measure starts with a question that asks the respondent to pick from a list of groups the one they liked the least (the list included atheists, homosexuals, Muslims, fascists, and communists).[8] Then respondents were asked a series of questions that assessed their tolerance of the groups, such as whether a person from that group should be "banned from being president" (see appendix B, questions 7 through 11 for the full list of questions used for this measure). Their responses to each of the questions were added together to create an intolerance score for each individual (the lower the score the more tolerant the individual). The average intolerance scores for Millennials who read all of the Harry Potter books versus those who didn't can be found in figure 3.4. Those who read all the books exhibited higher levels of tolerance than those who did not, and the difference between fans and nonfans existed with all measures of fandom.[9] So

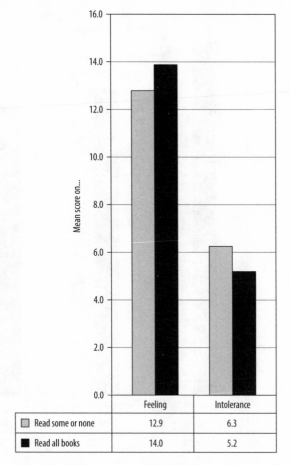

	Feeling	Intolerance
☐ Read some or none	12.9	6.3
◼ Read all books	14.0	5.2

Figure 3.4. Sum of feeling thermometer scores and tolerance scores by whether respondent read all of the Harry Potter books (ANOVA, F = 25.5, significant at the .000 level, for feeling thermometer scores; F = 23.2, significant at the .000 level, for the intolerance scale).

it seems that Harry Potter fans' attitudes reflect the tolerance practiced by the Potter protagonists.

To assess whether the series's attitudes about equality show up in Millennial Potter fans, we asked the question that the American National Elections Studies has long used to measure support for governmental

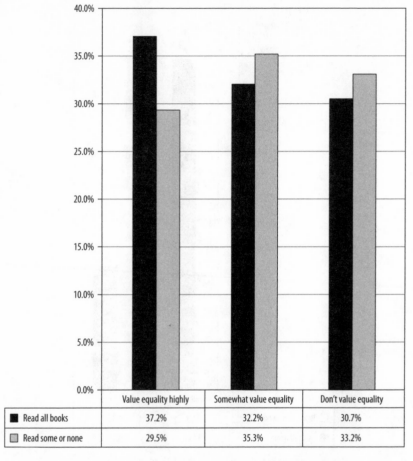

	Value equality highly	Somewhat value equality	Don't value equality
■ Read all books	37.2%	32.2%	30.7%
☐ Read some or none	29.5%	35.3%	33.2%

Figure 3.5. Whether respondent values equality, by Harry Potter fan (margin of error at 95% confidence level is ±2.9%).

promotion of equality. The question asks people to place themselves on a scale where one end represents those who believe government should see to it that everyone has a job and a good standard of living and the other end those who believe that government should just let each person get ahead on his or her own. The responses from fans and nonfans can be found in figure 3.5. It seems, at least with regard to believing equality is important enough for government to promote, that fans of Rowling's tale hold similar perspectives as the tale's heroes, expressing more support for government promotion of equality than nonfans (and this was true regardless of how we measured fandom).[10] In the words of one Millennial, "Along with most of the other entertainment media that I prefer, Harry Potter favors middle-class (or even lower-class), hard-working citizens. The contrast between the Weasley family and the Malfoy family is a prime example of how Rowling juxtaposes our traditional views on wealth and poverty. . . . Harry Potter implies that the poor, such as the Weasleys, are hard-working, but there is an injustice in the current system that does not reward hard work, but rewards business connections, old wealth, and 'pure blood.' This emphasis reinforced my political views that poverty is a societal issue and blame cannot be placed on the individual who is in poverty."[11]

Lesson 3: Don't Be an Authoritarian Git

Testing for differences between Potter fans and nonfans on the predisposition to authoritarianism (that is, the tendency to show obedience to authorities, to conform to rules and norms, and to disdain those not deemed part of the in-group) involved using a modified version of a measure of authoritarianism. Respondents were asked to choose between two words or phrases—independence and *respect for elders*, curiosity and *good manners*, *obedience* and self respect, considerate and *well behaved*—the option that appealed to them more (the italicized choices are the ones that those with a predisposition to authoritarianism would be more likely to choose).[12] We added up the total of the more authoritarian word choices selected by each respondent and compared Potter fans and nonfans on their scores. As hypothesized, Harry Potter fans scored significantly lower on the authoritarian predisposition (see fig. 3.6). Additionally, self-placement on the Harry Potter fan scale and respondents' scores on the trivia questions were correlated, as expected.[13] While those who saw all the movies scored lower on the authoritarian predisposition scale, the difference was too small for us to be confident that it was not due to chance.

Lesson 4: Violence and Torture Are Bad

Do the attitudes of Harry Potter fans on the use of deadly force and torture parallel the perspectives of the characters of the series? Yes, they do.

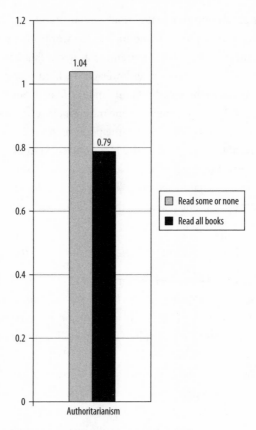

Figure 3.6. Mean score on authoritarian predisposition and whether respondent read all of the Harry Potter books (ANOVA, F = 16.4, significant at the .000 level).

We asked two questions to assess respondents' attitudes regarding the use of deadly force. One question asked whether the person favored or opposed the death penalty; the other asked whether they agreed or disagreed with the statement, "the best way to deal with the threat of terrorism is to hunt down and kill all the terrorists." The responses of Harry Potter fans and nonfans on these questions can be found in figure 3.7. Potter fans seem to reflect the series's lessons on the use of deadly force from the series, showing less support for the death penalty and disagree-

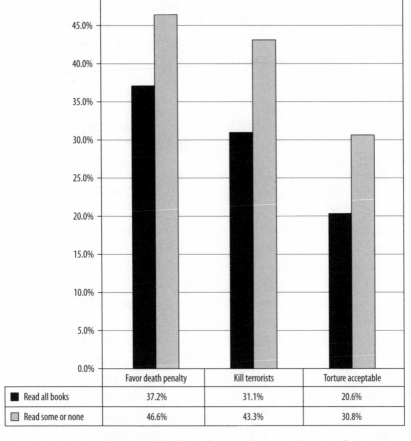

Figure 3.7. Attitudes toward deadly violence and torture (margin of error at 95% confidence level is ±2.9%).

ing with the statement that hunting down and killing terrorists is the best way to deal with the threat of terrorism.[14] In this case, those who saw all the movies only differed from those who didn't on the issue of the death penalty (and, not as dramatically, 39% of those who saw all the movies favored the death penalty compared to 47% of those who did not).

To see whether Potter fans differed from nonfans on the issue of torture, we asked, "Would you regard the use of torture against people suspected of involvement in terrorism as acceptable or unacceptable?" The responses are in figure 3.7. While 31 percent of nonfans found torture acceptable, only 21 percent of fans did. The difference could be seen where fandom was measured by trivia scores and the fan scale; however, fans of the movies did not differ on this question from those who did not see all the movies.

Lesson 5: Government Leaders Are Corrupt, Incompetent, and Fixated on Maintaining Power

Does the portrayal of politicians in the series show up in fans' views of real life politicians? Again, the answer is yes. We asked respondents, "Ultimately, how do you think historians will view the George W. Bush administration?" A greater percentage of Harry Potter fans than nonfans expressed the belief that historians will view the George W. Bush administration unfavorably (see fig. 3.8).[15] Overall, however, Potter fans proved to be more skeptical and less cynical than nonfans. We asked three questions to measure cynicism and added up the responses for a cynicism score.[16] The average cynicism scores for fans and nonfans are shown in figure 3.9. So, while Potter fans were more likely to think negatively of President Bush, they were, as we hypothesized, less cynical about the political system and more likely to evince a sense of personal efficacy.[17] These differences are reflected in a comparison of participation levels between fans and nonfans. We asked respondents if they had participated in different political activities—from voting to writing letters to government officials (see questions 21 through 28, and 30). As figure 3.9 shows, Harry Potter fans have participated in more political activities than nonfans, perhaps reflecting the story's lesson on the need to act, and efficacy of doing something to fight what is "wrong" in the world.[18]

The fact that all of the lessons of the Harry Potter series are reflected in the Millennial fans of the series perhaps helps explain why the Obama campaign message resonated so well with Millennials, two-thirds of whom voted for Obama in 2008.[19] As shown in figure 3.10, our survey found that Potter fans were more likely to have reported voting for Obama than were nonfans in 2008. Fifty-eight percent of those who read all of the books voted for Obama, versus 45 percent of those who did not. Addition-

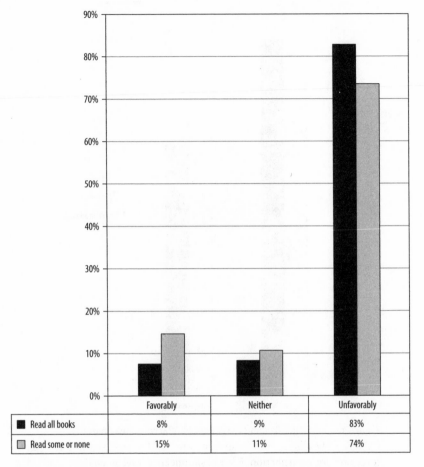

	Favorably	Neither	Unfavorably
■ Read all books	8%	9%	83%
□ Read some or none	15%	11%	74%

Figure 3.8. How historians will view Bush administration, by Harry Potter reader (margin of error at 95% confidence level is ±2.9%).

ally, fewer Potter fans than nonfans failed to vote.[20] Those who watched all the movies (as opposed to having read all the books) voted for Obama by a smaller margin.

Lesson 6: Be Skeptical, Not Cynical

The final hypothesis we tested had to do with whether fans were more likely to reflect the lessons in skepticism of the series. The story contains

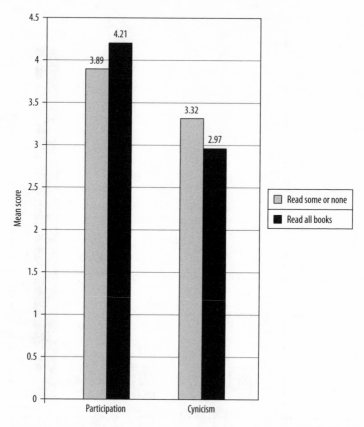

Figure 3.9. Participation and cynicism, by Harry Potter reader (ANOVA of differences of means for cynicism, F = 16.0, significance level .000, for participation, F = 7.0, significance level at .008).

enough twists to convince readers to be cautious that not everything is as it seems and to withhold judgment until the evidence is in, while, on the other hand, offering additional lessons not to succumb to cynicism. In order to get at the potential effect of those lessons, we developed a question meant to differentiate skeptics from cynics. The question was as follows: "Within our culture there exist theories that challenge the historical record or the consensus among the scientific community, such as the notion that the moon landing was fake, that global warming is a myth, that there was a conspiracy to assassinate JFK, and that the US government

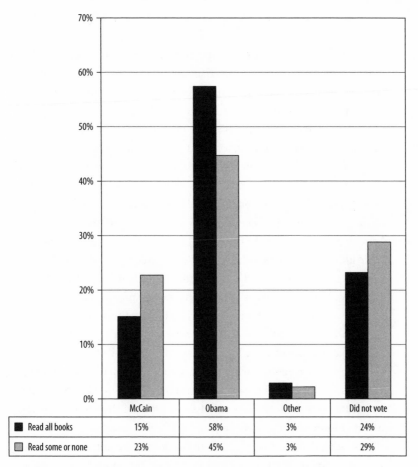

Figure 3.10. Vote for president in 2008, by Harry Potter reader.

staged the September 11th attacks. Which of the following describes your views of these theories that challenge the historical record or the consensus among the scientific community? I believe many of these theories. I believe one or two of these theories. I don't believe any of these theories." Skeptics, we believed, would be more likely to side with the evidence and reject the conspiracy theories. As hypothesized, Harry Potter fans were more likely to pick the skeptical responses to this question (44% of fans answered that they believed one or two of the conspiracy theories as compared to 52% of nonfans).

Conclusion

Overall, there is abundant evidence that Harry Potter fans are different from nonfans on the very subjects that were covered in the lessons of the series. While Harry Potter fans *are* different, and while the theories discussed above suggest that these differences could very well be due in part to the Harry Potter series, the evidence presented in this chapter is only suggestive of a Harry Potter effect. Just because two variables correlate (here, being a fan and certain political attitudes) doesn't mean one *caused* the other. Indeed, there are many possibilities for why two phenomena correlate other than causation. It could be coincidence (though, the consistency of our findings suggest otherwise). It could be that some other phenomenon is the cause of change in both of the observed variables. A classic illustration of this is the correlation between ice cream consumption and violent crime rates. Does consumption of ice cream cause violent crime? No. Warmer climates are instead a factor in both phenomena. A more personal example of this is that when I coach third base for my rec league baseball team, the team always seems to score runs. Do I cause this? Is that because of some luck or magic I possess? Unfortunately, no. It is because I am usually coaching third when the top of the batting order (which has all the best hitters on the team) is up (because I am one of the worst hitters on the team and bat at the bottom of the order). Consequently, a more sophisticated statistical analysis is called for in order to rule out other reasons that Harry Potter fans are different, reasons aside from the exposure to the politics of the series. There are several ways to run such an analysis, and in the next chapter we discuss how we went about doing so. From that analysis we find that the observed differences between Potter fans and nonfans cannot be explained away by other circumstances, though this still doesn't prove a causal relationship exists (causation between two variables can only truly be established using an experimental design). Additionally, the more sophisticated analysis we run shows that there is evidence to suggest that Rowling's world may have affected Millennials in different ways related to these political perspectives. For the details on this, turn to the next chapter.

CHAPTER FOUR

The Role of Harry Potter in the Political Development of Millennials

An appropriate (and appropriately skeptical) reaction to the material in the previous chapter could be "just because Harry Potter fans are different from nonfans doesn't mean that the story of the boy who lived caused those differences." Indeed, there are a host of alternative explanations for why Harry Potter fans might differ from nonfans on these matters, many of which we discussed in chapter 2. It could be that Potter fans were already accepting, tolerant, less disposed to authoritarianism, peaceful, liberal, politically active, and skeptical, or that they became so due to the influence of their families, school, or community. Or it could be that the political differences we observed are related to being an avid reader, and that being avid readers is what led some Millennials to Harry Potter. We have already proffered a series of sound responses that address these concerns and so argue that Rowling's tale affected Millennials from a theoretical perspective (see chap. 2). Here we bolster those arguments by putting the evidence from Millennials to a more rigorous test in order to statistically rule out alternative explanations for those findings. It is, ultimately, impossible to *prove* that the Harry Potter phenomenon caused fans to view politics in ways that reflect the lessons of the books (such proof could only come from a true experiment, which is impossible in testing the long-term and cumulative effects we have posited). But the results of the more rigorous statistical tests that we report on below, as well as the words of Millennials themselves on this issue, leave us confident that the story of the struggles of the wizarding world against Voldemort did indeed play an important role in the political development of many Millennials.

A More Complex Model of the Potter Effect

To statistically rule out some of the alternative explanations for why the political views of Harry Potter fans differ from nonfans, we included questions in the survey that measure those alternative explanations. We revisit each of the lessons of the series to discuss the questions and how the answers to them affected our findings. In the process we build a complex model of the development of Millennials' political views. A pared down summary of the model can be found in figure 4.1.

Lessons 1 and 2: Acceptance of Diversity and Political Tolerance

What, other than exposure to Harry Potter might explain the findings that Potter fans have more positive feelings toward out-groups (diversity) and show a higher level of political tolerance than nonfans? According to Karen Stenner's work, the most important predictor of hostility toward out-groups and political intolerance is the authoritarian dynamic (which, attentive readers will note, was also associated with being a fan of Harry Potter; this additional complexity in the effect of fandom is discussed below).[1] People with the authoritarian predisposition are, under conditions of threat to the social order, the ones who exhibit discriminatory and intolerant attitudes. While we could not manipulate the threat level, we did measure the authoritarian predisposition and controlled for it when we tested the relationship between Potter fan levels and feelings toward diversity and political tolerance.

To "control for" another factor statistically means testing for whether a relationship between two variables is detectable regardless of the value of other variables. For purposes of illustration, let's say that the control variable, in this case the authoritarian predisposition, can be split into two categories, authoritarian and not authoritarian.[2] Statistically controlling for authoritarianism in this hypothetical means that the analysis looks for a relationship between the measure of Harry Potter fandom and political tolerance among those who are categorized as authoritarians and those who were not, separately. If the procedure finds a relationship between being a Potter fan and tolerance among authoritarians and among those who are not authoritarians then it can be said that being a Potter fan was associated with greater tolerance regardless of whether respondents were authoritarians. In this way, it allows us to statistically rule out alternative explanations of the relationship between being a Potter fan and political views because the relationship, if it is still evident after such tests, exists regardless of other characteristics of our respondents. We perform this analysis for all of the relationships we examine.

When looking for alternative explanations for feelings toward diverse groups and political tolerance, it could be argued that the study should also include a measure of ideology, since in many people's minds negative attitudes about diversity and tolerance are associated with conservatism. As it turns out, that is not entirely true. There are different kinds of conservatives—status quo conservatives, laissez-faire conservatives, and those who are predisposed to authoritarianism. It is those who are predisposed to authoritarianism who evince negative attitudes toward outgroups, not conservatives in general.[3] Additionally, people on the left can be authoritarians, too. Consequently, the authoritarian predisposition is superior to a general measure of ideology for predicting acceptance of diversity and tolerance, so it is the one we use here.

In addition to the authoritarian measure, we also control for background characteristics—race, gender, whether the respondent grew up in a city, and whether the respondent was a student of the University of Vermont (both because of its liberal reputation and because its students composed a large portion of the sample). In order to consider the possibility that the Potter effect was due to parental influence expressed through an encouragement to read the books, we asked respondents to tell us what role their parents played in their decision to read the Harry Potter series. We utilize the responses to this question for an additional test, running the analysis of the relationships between Potter fandom and acceptance of diversity and tolerance only for those whose parents did not encourage them to read the books.

After running the analysis with all of these control variables, we found that Harry Potter fans are still more accepting of diversity and more politically tolerant regardless of these other characteristics of respondents (for the numerical results of this analysis, see appendix C). This is true even when we drop out all of the Potter fans whose parents encouraged them to read the books. The results of these more vigorous tests allow us to rule out some of the major alternative explanations for why Potter fans are more accepting and tolerant, and, ultimately, they give us a greater level of confidence that the story of the boy who lived played a role in the development of these attitudes among Millennials. That Harry Potter influenced feelings about diversity and tolerance is evident in the comments of Millennials:

> I guess because seeing how certain creatures were definitely discriminated against and marginalized, and Harry always seemed to have personal relationships with all of them, I definitely took that away in the way you would think—to not be judgmental, and to be open to people.[4]

> There is obvious racism in the series, but it's not against people's race, i.e., African, Asian, etc., but against the makeup of wizard blood. The slurs "mud-blood" are thrown around, usually by the Slytherins, as an insult against a wizard's family heritage, or lack of. Hermione is subject to this harsh treatment because she is "muggle born" and was selected to attend Hogwarts because she is obviously a very smart and intuitive girl. . . . I think this has developed a degree of tolerance in my own political socialization.[5]

> Harry Potter also addressed the treatment of people who are different from oneself. This was important I think because though my family was always very liberal and highly accepting of diversity, there is very little diversity [where I grew up], particularly racial diversity. Having such issues addressed in popular culture reinforce[s] the idea [of accepting diversity].[6]

Following a discussion of Hermione's activism on behalf of house-elves, one respondent was asked if Hermione's activism inspired her to be more like Hermione, to which the fan replied, "Yeah, that's something that the three main characters do a lot. And because they do that, it made me want to do that too. And they were doing important things and they were just kids. So it made me want to do it, too."[7] Note the last part of that quote also supports the notion that Harry Potter affected fans' sense of themselves as being effectively involved in politics. After a discussion of how Hermione was persecuted for being Muggle-born, one fan said, "I definitely took things away from that and applied them to how I feel about, I guess, minorities and just groups of people that are discriminated against in the first place."[8]

Lesson 3: Authoritarianism

What, other than being a fan of Harry Potter, could explain fans' lower scores on the authoritarian predisposition measure? Again we turn to Karen Stenner for her insightful work on authoritarianism. In her research on the matter, Stenner found only two significant factors that seemed to explain people's level of authoritarianism—the cognitive skills necessary to deal with complexity and openness to experience.[9] So we followed her lead. To measure cognitive skills, we asked, "Outside of the books you were assigned for school, what kind of reader were you when you were younger?" As shown earlier, being an avid reader has been found to be associated with higher cognitive skills. Since we know that a large portion of our sample (17%) said that Harry Potter made readers out of them, including the responses to this question about the type of reader they consider themselves has the added benefit of allowing us to test for a possible indirect effect of Harry Potter on some of the political attitudes we assessed. We measure openness to experience by asking respondents, as Stenner did, to agree or disagree with statements about themselves such as "If I feel my mind starting to drift off into daydreams, I usually get busy and start concentrating on some work or activity instead" (see questions 59, 62, and 63 in appendix B for the rest). We also controlled for the level of education attained by the respondents' fathers.[10]

The results of the more sophisticated analysis show that being a Harry Potter fan (as measured by how many of the books respondents read) was associated with lower scores on the authoritarian predisposition measure regardless of whether the respondents were readers, their openness to experience, or their fathers' education levels. This was true as well for the segment of the sample whose parents did not encourage them to read the books. The role Harry Potter played in predisposition to authoritarianism also came out the Millennials' own words as they discussed the books.

The Harry Potter books appealed to me because at the time I was reading the series I was about the same age as the characters of the books.
Therefore, I could really [relate] with some of the (non-magic-related)
challenges they faced. . . . While I did not consciously try to imitate the
characters from Harry Potter, I seemed to, roughly, behave the same
way. I was often the only one of my peers that was willing to take a
stand against the teacher when we thought we were being treated un-
fairly. I tried to be diplomatic and non-confrontational before jumping
head first into the proverbial fire. I believe I dealt with authority figures
much like the main characters in Harry Potter handled challenges to
their independence from those in power, as in the case with Professor
Umbridge, for example.[11]

[T]o see all the parts when they'd all say things in class, like to Snape or
something. And you'd be like "oh my gosh" they're actually saying that
to their teacher! That's cool, I could do that! You know, just not to accept what you're told without saying anything.[12]

Explaining why some people are more likely to be predisposed to authoritarianism is difficult, as Stenner showed. This fact is reflected in the
limited amount of variation explained by being a fan of Harry Potter (that
is, while the relationship is statistically significant, the magnitude of the
effect of being a fan, while important, is not that great). It is also shown
in the amount of variation in this predisposition explained by the model
as a whole (as measured by the R-square in table C.1). To a certain degree,
such results are to be expected given Stenner's findings and the fact that
most media effects, when measured, are not overly large, which makes
sense given that a broad combination of factors shape people's views.[13]
Nonetheless, the fact a book series read for entertainment adds a bit to
our understanding of why some people are more or less predisposed to
authoritarianism when controlling for other known factors indicates that
entertainment media can play a role in such an important predisposition
for a democratic society.

Lesson 4: Violence and Torture

Other than being a Potter fan, what factors could explain differences in attitudes toward the deadly use of force or torture? Given that the political environment at the time Harry Potter was so popular was one in which conservatives were the most ardent defenders of the use of deadly force and of interrogation methods many labeled as torture, we thought that a key factor to control for would be ideology. So we asked respondents to place themselves on a five-point ideological scale ranging from "very liberal" to "very conservative." Since those who are predisposed toward authoritarianism are more likely to support punitive responses to violations of the social order, we included the measure of authoritarianism in the model as well. Additionally, we controlled for another alternative explanation (and a possible indirect effect of the Harry Potter series) by including the respondents' feelings toward the diverse groups we presented to them. The thinking was that less warmth of feeling may be associated with a greater willingness to use deadly force and torture.

For this analysis we combined answers to the deadly force and torture questions to create a scale of views about violence and torture. Then we tested to see whether Harry Potter fandom was related to views about violence regardless of ideology, authoritarianism, and feelings toward diverse groups. It was. Fans of Harry Potter were less supportive of deadly force and torture even when considering other characteristics of respondents. This was true as well for the segment of the sample whose parents did not encourage them to read the books.

> Interviewer: It's the end of the seventh book. I'm Voldemort, you're Harry, we are pointing our wands at each other. Would you go for the killing curse or the disarming curse? Not knowing how it plays out.

> HP Fan: I guess, I think if I were Harry in that situation, because that's what Harry does, then yeah, I would have done that [used a disarming curse instead of the killing curse], because he was trying to like stay true to what he had always said. And that he wasn't just going to kill someone just because they were in his way. And everyone was like you can't use that spell [disarming] because if someone hears you then they'll know it's you and you're the only one that does that. And he's like

well I'm not just going to torture or kill someone because they're in my way.

Lessons 5 and 6: Cynicism, Participation, and Skepticism

Ruling out alternative explanations for levels of cynicism involved controlling for partisanship and whether the respondent was an avid reader. Partisans, we expected, would be less cynical than independents. Those who are readers are more likely to develop a clearer understanding of what happens in government and politics and thus also are likely to be less cynical. With these factors controlled for, the negative relationship between being a Harry Potter fan and cynicism is still evident. This was true of the whole sample and of those whose parents had not encouraged them to read the series.

We measured factors commonly used to explain levels of political participation, including the level of partisanship (those with stronger ties to either party are more likely to participate in politics), political efficacy (those who are confident in their ability to have an impact on politics are more likely to be involved in politics), and cynicism (expecting those who are cynical would be less likely to participate). We also included a control for whether the individual was a political science major or minor (for obvious reasons). The analysis that includes all these controls still finds that being a Harry Potter fan is associated with higher levels of participation whether we consider all respondents or just those whose parents played no role in reading Harry Potter.

Finally, we controlled for respondents' level of internal political efficacy to further test the relationship between being a Harry Potter fan and our measure of skepticism. We thought that those with lower levels of efficacy would be more likely to buy into conspiracy theories—since conspiracy theories can make the world easier to understand and provide an excuse for not trying to do anything about politics. The association between being a fan and skepticism exists regardless of respondents' levels of internal political efficacy and for those whose parents did not encourage them to read the books, as well as for the entire sample.

Our second look at the relationship between being a Harry Potter fan and how respondents thought historians would judge the Bush administration (not depicted in fig. 4.1 in order to avoid making it too complicated) involved controlling for partisanship and ideology. After doing that, Harry Potter fans were only slightly more likely to think the Bush administration would be viewed unfavorably. On the other hand, even after controlling for party and ideology, Potter fans *were* more likely to vote for Barack Obama in the 2008 election.[14] This was true even when we just focused on those whose parents did not encourage them to read the books.

Harry Potter fans, it seems, are likely to be less cynical and more skeptical than nonfans; they also are more likely to participate in politics and were more likely to vote for Obama in 2008. These relationships were evident regardless of other characteristics known to affect cynicism, participation, and vote choices. Having ruled out some of the major alternative explanations, we can feel a bit more confident in asserting that the relationship between being a Potter fan and these political perspectives is not just a coincidence or a product of some other factor. In interviews with fans, most attributed their views on government to the Harry Potter series. Take the following conversation, for example:

Interviewer: I'm just wondering if there's anything you see that could have come from the series in yourself?

HP Fan: Um, I feel like, this is kind of weird, but an awareness about corruption in government. Because I feel like the way their government is set up, I guess it seems to be like the past was often good but then there are so many times when it's super corrupt and so I feel like, I don't know, and then if something were to happen in the United States government, which is also often corrupt but to a different sort of extent. But, I think that maybe people who like, were aware of it, in the way that reading would, sort of, react to it faster?

Interviewer: So you think that sort of taught you early on to be aware, or have heads up to government being imperfect?

HP Fan: Yeah, I mean I think a lot of times in elementary school, especially, like the way that you view the United States government is kind of, not like wrong, but I feel like they try to make it seem better than it is.

On the issue of skepticism versus cynicism, this is another fan's account:

> HP Fan: I meet with a bunch of friends every Tuesday night, and we just talk about what's going on, and usually it always boils down to politics and how we're handling things. I mean Libya being one on the page right now. But, I definitely am critical, or skeptical I guess, but not so skeptical that I'm cynical. I mean I'm critical, but I'm definitely not cynical.

> Interviewer: No, because you still vote, you're a political science major, you still care,

> HP Fan: Yeah, totally. I also kind of just have this faith in government, and maybe it's misplaced.

> Interviewer: Do you think any of those views could have come from HP?

> HP Fan: I would not be surprised, it played such a huge part in my life, and just the amount of times that I've read them and had those kind of values beat into my head. Then I definitely see that as, I mean because my family's not, I find myself very different from my family in terms of the way that I view government, and the way I view politics in general. And that could have something to do with it.

Pulling It All Together

The overall picture of what we have found regarding Harry Potter and the politics of Millennials is mapped out in figure 4.1. The width of the arrows represents the magnitude of the relationships between each of the characteristics depicted in the model. (The full equations behind this model can be found in appendix C and the model with the coefficients included can be found in appendix D.)

In addition to summarizing the findings of the survey, figure 4.1 illustrates one additional aspect of the Harry Potter effect—the indirect effects the series had on fans' political views. Harry Potter fandom appears to have had an effect not only on the political views associated with the lessons of the series but also on some of the antecedents of those political views. Take the relationship between being a fan and being a reader, for

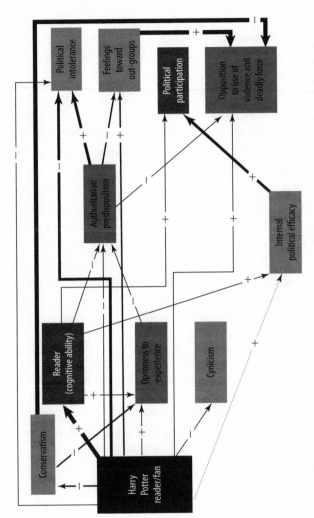

Figure 4.1. Direct and indirect effects of Harry Potter (lines represent relationships—the thicker the line the stronger the relationship; direction of the relationship is indicated by a + or −).

example. Survey responses tell us that the story of the boy wizard made readers out of many Millennials (17% told us, "I was not much of a reader until I read the Harry Potter series, but after reading Harry Potter I began to read more books"). And being a reader was associated with lower scores on the authoritarian predisposition and a higher level of internal political efficacy. Thus, the Harry Potter phenomenon seems to have influenced the levels of authoritarianism and efficacy of Millennials not just directly but also indirectly by enticing Millennials to read.

Note also that the relationship between being a Potter fan and acceptance of diversity and tolerance operates not just directly but also through authoritarianism. Being a fan of the series is associated with warmer feelings toward out-groups and lower levels of the authoritarian predisposition. Lower levels of authoritarianism are in turn associated with warmer feelings toward out-groups. Furthermore, Potter fans are more open to experience, which in turn is associated with a lower predisposition to authoritarianism.

Other evidence suggesting indirect effects includes relationships between Potter fandom, being a reader, and internal political efficacy, which is in turn related to levels of participation. And being a fan of the series is associated with being more liberal, which is then associated with greater opposition to the use of deadly force and torture.

All told, the analysis finds many relationships between being a fan of Harry Potter and the political views that correspond with the lessons of the series (trace all the lines in fig. 4.1 to review all of these effects). These relationships have held up to more vigorous statistical tests and suggest that the tale of the boy wizard had a multifaceted effect (possible direct and indirect effects) on the political development of many Millennials. There are more sophisticated statistical procedures we would like to run in order to enhance the rigor of the analysis and increase the confidence of the findings, but unfortunately they are not possible due to limitations of the data collected.[15]

Conclusion

As noted, there are more sophisticated tests and alternative methods than the ones used here to test for the Harry Potter effect. Such tests and methods could be used to rule out additional alternative explanations for why Harry Potter Millennial fans differ from the rest of their generation on the political views related to the lessons of the series. These approaches would require the measurement of other characteristics of respondents in order to offer more fully specified models of people's attitudes or different overall research designs (such as experiments or longitudinal studies) that could establish causation or measure the political variables over time. We will have to leave such approaches to future studies that we hope will follow on the findings of our research.

That said, the mix of a strong theoretical basis, the consistency of our findings, and the qualitative data we obtained make us confident that the Harry Potter series did play an important role in the political development of those Millennials who became fans.

To conclude this chapter we would like to turn again to the words of Millennials themselves. Were you to ask fans of Harry Potter directly whether the series affected their political development, the initial reaction of most might be to deny that it did. Indeed, we suspect that perhaps many of you who picked up this book were also highly skeptical at first. But as we found in our interviews (and maybe upon reading, you have found as well), as the discussion of the story of the boy who lived and the political lessons contained within really gets going, it dawns on fans that Harry Potter did indeed have an effect on how they see the world. That has been the experience we have shared with fans, as the quotes throughout this book have demonstrated. Indeed, all the Potter fans that were interviewed by their fellow students believed that the series had an influence on the way they view politics, either independently or in a way that reinforced the effect of other agents of socialization.

> But how did all of this shape my views of what was really going on in the world around me? I understood after my eleventh birthday that I was in fact not a wizard and at that point the last vestige of belief in a wizarding society hidden within our own vanished, as a matter of fact it was just plain ridiculous. But all of the morals that I took away from the book gave me a much more profound understanding of wrong and right than any Sunday school class I ever attended. What Harry did for me as I was growing up was to provide me with a template for human

interactions that I could refer to as I struggled through different social situations. He was more than a good friend because I knew all of his thoughts and inner secrets[;] he showed me examples of when to be respectful, when to rebel, how to be gracious, how to resolve conflicts with friends and foes alike.

But Harry was one of many[;] Batman, the Ninja Turtles, Calvin & Hobb[e]s, all attempted to teach me similar lessons[,] but for some reason a story such as Harry's connects to my perceptions on an entirely different level.[16]

[T]here is no doubt in my mind that the movies, TV shows and books [including Harry Potter] I chose to watch and read had a direct effect on my political views. I thought for a while that it was more just reinforcing the views my parents had instilled in me. After going back for winter break though I realized I don't agree with my parents all of the time and don't have the same world view as them. The only other source I can conclude I got it from is the media.[17]

I have grown up with these books and films and while I do not see Harry Potter as being the main source of my political socialization or the main influence on my political affiliation or views, I do see that it has helped to bolster previous views I held that were implanted via other entertainment that my parents subjected me to.[18]

In beginning to think more deeply about Harry Potter I was somewhat surprised at how much political content emerged. The main themes that affected me concern identity [student was of mixed race background who related to Harry's "half-breed" status] and ideology formation, and the ability we have to form community in order to fight against potentially oppressive politics, government, and power.[19]

I had a great love of film and went to the movies with my friends almost every weekend. I was in middle school when the Lord of the Rings films first came out, and I remember being struck with the sentiment of it. The story resounded with me greatly: a (quite literally) small person leaving the comforts of an idyllic home to fight forces of evil and destruction, aided by an apparently random group of companions. In retrospect, perhaps Tolkien and Jackson first charted my path towards radicalism. The Harry Potter world was similarly attractive and instilled many of the same values, with a perhaps greater emphasis on nonviolence. In each of these stories, loyal friends were a key feature and ultimately indispensible in accomplishing the final goals. Thus, I realized that struggle for one's values was important, but that it would be difficult to do so alone. In addition to this, the Harry Potter books made me an avid reader.[20]

I am a Harry Potter fanatic. I have read the entire series at least seven times (and have probably read number three closer to ten times). The characters that make the series so easy to read over and over again are all of the characters that have traits that I wish to be able to emulate in my life.[21]

I've been reading Harry Potter since it was first published (I even attended the release of the second book when I was six years old). I would only embarrass myself if I conceded the amount of times I've read and reread the books. As a super-fan, I've had many deep discussions on Harry Potter, and I've learned more than the overt political messages of the books (Fudge and Scrimgeour's administrations, for example). I am interested in the values J. K. Rowling preaches. Through my numerous readings of Harry Potter I've learned what tolerance, loyalty, and courage truly are.[22]

I cannot remember any shows or movies I watched, or books I read in my youth, that had a strong female protagonist. Hermione Granger, the lead female character in the Harry Potter series, was like me. She liked to read, she liked to write, she loved to learn. She was smart, she was confident, and she grew in to her beauty. I dressed up as her for Halloween after the first book came out. . . . I do believe I share some of the characteristics of the "Harry Potter Generation" that the article talks about, and the more I think about it the more I feel I fit those categories. I love Harry Potter and have so much of my childhood and myself invested within those pages. It truly is a magical experience for my generation, and hopefully for generations to come.[23]

Fiction, Reality, and Politics

The story of the boy who lived takes place within both our world and a world of magic. That world of magic is hidden from us Muggles, but it exists nonetheless, just beyond our reach . . . perhaps somewhere between platforms 9 and 10? Those with magical abilities, whether they grew up in a wizarding or Muggle household, receive their letter inviting them to Hogwarts School of Witchcraft and Wizardry when they are eleven years old; those without those abilities live their lives in ignorance of the magic that is all around. The purpose of this book has been to show that the tale of the boy wizard contains yet another hidden world—one of politics—and to explore how that hidden world has the power to transform those who are drawn in by the magic of the books. The politics in Harry Potter's world are embedded in the nature of its heroes (Harry's openness and tolerance) and its villains (Umbridge's authoritarianism), in the lessons that the characters learn as they move through the tale (that things are not always what they seem, that politicians can be bungling, incompetent, and corrupt), and in those revealed through plot devices and twists in the story line (that one can defeat an enemy without resorting to violence and deadly force).

When we become immersed in a story, we are moved to emulate the characteristics of the heroes and reject those of the villains. When we become immersed, we truly experience all that the fictional world offers and take to heart the lessons that our heroes learn. In doing so, we internalize those characteristics and lessons in ways that can shape our politics. Like the heroes in the tale, we have found that fans of Harry Potter are more tolerant and accepting of differences, less authoritarian, and less likely to view torture or the use of deadly force as appropriate than nonfans. Potter fans viewed the Bush administration with the skepticism that the incompetent and corrupt politicians of the Ministry of Magic deserved (more so than nonfans). And from this sense of skepticism (as opposed to cynicism), fans were more likely than nonfans to demonstrate a higher level of confidence that they can influence their political world and were more likely to do something to try to change their world, as Harry's and his friends' struggles and triumphs demonstrated was possible.

Harry Potter was just one of many factors that went into the political development of the Millennial Generation. Nonetheless, the consistent differences between fans and nonfans on perspectives that parallel the political lessons of the story (differences that remain even after taking into consideration alternate explanations) suggest that the Potter tale played a role in shaping the political perspectives of Millennials who became fans. Such findings should not be surprising given that the Harry Potter phenomenon so captivated a large segment of the generation during their most politically vulnerable and formative years. Whether it provided new perspectives or reinforced those already in their world, the deep immersion in the story and identification with the characters almost guaranteed an alignment of fans' perspectives with those of the wizarding world, perspectives that would differentiate them from their nonfan peers. Additionally, that Harry Potter enticed a substantial portion of Millennials to become readers has had, and will likely continue to have, a cascading effect on other political characteristics of the generational unit comprised of Harry Potter's Muggle fans.

The lesson of this book, however, goes beyond the influence of the tale of the boy who lived. Fiction—whether found in books, films, television shows, or video games—has the power to shape our politics. All stories contain lessons we may learn; all characters in those stories have traits and values we may try to emulate. The effect of fictional stories on politics is largely uncharted territory for social science research. While there are many methodological challenges to finding out when and how fiction shapes politics, the deeper understanding of the origin of citizens' perspectives on politics that it offers makes it worth tackling those challenges.

One of the biggest challenges to such research is the notion that we are selective in the political messages we allow ourselves to be expose to. We *do* tend to be drawn to the stories whose lessons resonate with us and whose characters remind us of ourselves or whom we want to be. As the C. S. Lewis character of the film *Shadowlands* says, "We read to know that we are not alone." Such experiences, however, are not unimportant when it comes to the nature of our political perspectives—they help to reinforce our perspectives and empower them in ways that make stories important. Feeling that we are not alone because we find that we share our thoughts, desires, and perspectives with at least one other person (especially if that person is the hero of a story we enjoy), after all, *does* give us greater confidence in ourselves and our views.

But we are not always so selective in the entertainment we choose. Blockbuster movies like *Avatar* attract millions for special effects that make the telling of a story that takes place on a distant world in the future seem real and thrilling to us. We also watch movies and television shows that our families or roommates choose; we join them to keep them company or just because a show is on; we get drawn in for any of a number of reasons (like the need for a good laugh) and as a result we are exposed to different perspectives. Or we watch or read things because our friends or family are discussing them and we want to take part in the conversation.[1] Since we are watching for fun and not for the conscious purpose of acquiring political information, our political defenses are down, opening the door to incidental learning of different political perspectives. We read books for our book clubs or because a bookstore clerk or an Amazon.com algorithm recommends a title to us, oftentimes for reasons that have nothing to do with the politically relevant perspectives contained within the story.[2] If we become immersed in those books because of their compelling stories or the interesting lives of the characters, we potentially expose ourselves to other perspectives that we may internalize.

We may also be drawn to characters that are like us in some ways but not in others, or who do things we would like to do that may have nothing to do with values or perspectives—like travel through all of space-time in a blue box, like the Doctor in *Doctor Who*. In such cases, do we not emulate some of these characters' other traits as well? And in the end, we become a composite of those in our worlds, real and imaginary, whom we admire and model ourselves after. You can find bits of Larry Darrel (protagonist of *The Razor's Edge*), the Doctor (he wishes, anyway), T. S. Garp, Legolas, Farimir, Artos (protagonist of *Sword at Sunset*) and *Star Trek* captains Kirk and Picard in one of the co-authors; Princess Leia, Kara Thrace (of *Battlestar Galactica*), and Sioned (a protagonist in the Dragon Prince series) in the other. Look within yourselves. Which characters' traits re-side there? Is Harry there? Hermione? Ron? Neville? You might surprise yourself with how many traits within you derive from fictional characters.

Finally, stories that come in series (or inspire never-ending sequels) can shift perspectives over time; if we are along for the ride, we might shift our perspectives as well. In the re-imagined *Battlestar Galactica* series, for example, the first season's portrayal of the Cylons as genocidal robots encourages intolerance and support for any sort of violence against them. By the fourth season, the human protagonists have allied themselves with some of the Cylons, and the line between Cylon and human blurs significantly, with love and eventually children shared between them. The Cylons are ultimately portrayed as just as human as the humans. These transformations over the course of the series are done in ways that can only engender greater tolerance. In the original *Star Wars*, the lines between good and evil are starkly drawn, and Darth Vader is pure, unredeemable evil, but by the third installment, the *Return of the Jedi*, the story proves that there is some good even in one of the classic villains of all time, Vader. A decade or so later, the full tragedy of Anakin Skywalker, aka Darth Vader, was told in Episodes I to III, completing his transformation from evil villain to tragic figure.

All of this is to say that if you want to understand where people are coming from politically, you need to go beyond what they watch, listen to, or read for news. You have to go beyond what they learn from agents of socialization that live and breathe. For a more complete understanding of why people develop the way that they do politically, it is vitally important that we understand what they do for *entertainment* as well. Do they read for fun? And what they read? What movies or television shows do they watch? Which video games do they play? In the process of reading, watching, or playing, we all become part of the world we involved ourselves in and it becomes part of us. As one fan said in response to a question about which Harry Potter book was her favorite,

> I would have to say the seventh probably. The fourth really had an impact on me at the time when it came out, but in terms of a book I'd say that the seventh was definitely my favorite. Because it has to do with the fact that you've been with them through everything, this is kind of the end point, what it's all been building up to, and you can see

how they are reacting in that situation. And it's very mature, and the way that it deals with things. And, things that are very human come out, like Ron leaving Harry and getting jealous of him and Hermione. And going off on your own, being scared and not knowing what you're doing. It's very . . . it speaks to people. It can speak to people at all moments of their lives.[3]

Do you want to share your experience with Harry Potter or any other books, shows, or movies? If so, visit www.harrypotterandthemillennials.com.

Research Methodology

Survey Methodology

The survey consisted of captive samples of college and university students from around the country and included a variety of schools that offer regional and class representation. The schools included a community college in New York (Adirondack Community College), an elite southern school (University of Mississippi), a second-tier southern school (Mississippi State University), an elite New England School (University of Vermont), two schools on the West Coast (California Polytechnic State University and Pacific Lutheran University), and a Midwest school (Iowa State University). For a breakdown of the sample by school, see table A.1.

After several rounds of work on the survey, we ran a pretest of it in POLS230, Vermont Legislative Research Service, at the University of Vermont. It was then put in the field in two waves (one in spring 2009 and one in fall 2009). The representativeness of the sample is indicated by the fact that the findings did not change between the two waves of the survey (though the increased size did provide better results in the tests for statistical significance). The survey was administered in classes in a variety of departments and at all levels of undergraduate courses. At the University of Vermont, POLS237, Film, TV and Public Opinion, students (the same students who helped design this project) were encouraged to ask permission to give the survey in classes of a variety of subjects and sizes; the surveys conducted at other schools were mainly in political science courses (a majority of respondents were political science majors or minors, as reported in table A.2). Before taking the survey, respondents heard the fol-

TABLE A.1
Sample Size by School

	Frequency	Percent
Mississippi State University	180	15.8
University of Vermont Film Showing	42	3.7
University of Vermont Spring 2009	273	23.9
University of Mississippi	57	5.0
California Polytechnic State University	91	8.0
Iowa State	30	2.6
Adirondack Community College	157	13.8
University of Vermont Fall 2009	279	24.5
Pacific Lutheran	32	2.8
Total	1,141	100.0

lowing script: "Students at University of Vermont under the supervision of a professor there are conducting a research project and have asked for our help. What they are asking is for us to fill out a survey that asks about your feelings on certain political issues and also some questions regarding the Harry Potter series. They would really appreciate it if you took the time to answer the survey honestly; it shouldn't take more than 15 minutes to complete it. Your responses will remain completely anonymous. To remain anonymous, you should NOT put your name on the answer sheet or survey. They thank you for doing this." The script's initial sentence was different for the classes surveyed at the University of Vermont. There, students ran the survey and introduced themselves as researchers working with their professor. The questionnaire was ordered so that it asked respondents the questions measuring the key political dependent variables before asking them about their exposure to the Harry Potter series.

The captive sample method (administering the survey to students in classes) ensures an excellent response rate and, if done properly, a diverse and representative sample of college students (who are the target population for this study). Captive samples of college students have been used in research that has been published in peer-reviewed journals (regarding the effects on entertainment media akin to this research, see Baumgartner and Morris, "*Daily Show* Effect," and Sester and Green, "You Are Who You Watch."

In addition to exercising caution in developing the sample, we also collected responses on control variables that allow for a more vigorous

TABLE A.2
Survey Demographics
(percentage of respondents)

Gender	
Male	53
Female	46
Race	
White	84
Black	6
American Indian	1
Asian	3
Mixed race	6
Hispanic	
Hispanic/Latino(a)	3
Not Hispanic/Latino(a)	94
Mixed	3
Place grew up	
Large city	10
Suburbia	36
Small city	24
Rural	30
Father's education level	
H.S. or less	22
Some college	21
B.A.	30
Professional degree	25
Don't know	3
Political science major or minor?	
Yes	51

test of the findings. Included among these variables was whether the respondents were political science majors or minors, to address the concern that many of the classes in which the survey was run were political science courses. We also added a variable to identify the school where the survey ran; we utilized this variable to control for the effects that the largest portion of the sample came from the University of Vermont (while we checked the impact of this variable for all of the regression equations reported in appendix C, we left it in the final models only where it had an effect or was theoretically expected to have an effect).

Personal Interviews and Essays

While the survey allows us to make some generalizations about Millennials in college and suggests a link between the Harry Potter series and political perspectives, it cannot provide proof that Harry Potter caused the differences in the perspectives that we found. To strengthen the case (albeit in a manner that still falls short of proving causation), we collected information from Millennials discussing the history of their political views and the role the story of the boy who lived played in the development of their views. This was done through personal interviews and introspective essays.

One set of personal interviews was conducted by students in POLS237, Film, TV and Public Opinion, using fellow University of Vermont students as their subjects. Subjects were recruited with flyers posted around campus asking for sixty to ninety minutes and offering a free pint of Ben & Jerry's ice cream for participation. All subjects were told that their responses would remain anonymous. Ten fans were interviewed this way. University of Vermont undergraduate Julie Seger conducted a second set of interviews for her undergraduate honors thesis (for which Gierzynski was thesis adviser). Seger recruited subjects by offering twenty-dollar gift cards and took a different approach to the interviews. First, to encourage subjects to open up, she discussed the results of the Harry Potter survey and her own experience with the Harry Potter series and how it affected her. She then had a general discussion of the books, the movies, and characters, during which, at appropriate points, she would ask the fan whether they thought the lessons of Harry Potter affected their views. Ten students participated.

Additional qualitative data was collected via personal essays assignments. Each semester, I ask students in my introductory course on the American political system, an intermediate-level course on the media and politics, and my research seminar to write introspective essays about their political socialization. In the essay assignment, students are encouraged to think about all of the socialization agents that may have played a role in shaping their political perspectives, to

> spend some time contemplating your own political socialization, thinking about how the mass media you have been exposed to in your life— entertainment media as well as news media—may have shaped your political views and/or politically relevant values (think broadly here, not just ideology or partisanship, but also important politically relevant

values such as, equality, tolerance, individualism, cynicism, etc., and your views on specific issues, such as abortion, the environment, foreign policy, etc.). In the process of thinking about this, think about the places you were exposed to representations of government and politics in the media (again, thinking broadly here . . . representations of politics and government do not have to be explicit or about the US system . . . they can be more subtle and about any governmental system, even those from a long time ago in a galaxy far, far away . . .).

Answers to the Harry Potter trivia questions from chapter 3:

1. The Half-Blood Prince was Severus Snape.
2. Peeves was a troublesome poltergeist at Hogwarts.
3. Ron's position in Quidditch was the Keeper.
4. The magical spells that wards off Dementor attacks is Expecto Patronum.
5. The vanishing cabinet connects Hogwarts to Borgin & Burke's.

The Questionnaire

Thank you for agreeing to take part in our class research project. Your participation and honest opinions are of utmost importance to the success of our research and will remain completely anonymous. Please answer the following questions by filling out the bubble on the scan form for the option that best fits what you think and feel.

Below are 4 pairs of words. Please choose the word that appeals to you more or that sounds better to you.

1. Independence or respect for elders	Independence	Respect for elders
2. Curiosity or good manners	Curiosity	Good manners
3. Obedience or self-respect	Obedience	Self-respect
4. Being considerate or well-behaved	Considerate	Well-behaved

5. Some people feel the government in Washington should see to it that every person has a job and a good standard of living. Suppose these people are at one end of a scale, at point "a." Others think the government should just let each person get ahead on their own. Suppose these people are at the other end, at point "e." And, of course, some other people have opinions somewhere in between. Where would you place YOURSELF on this scale?

a. Government should see to job and standard of living.	b.	c.	d.	e. Government should just let each person get ahead on their own.

6. If you had to pick, which of the following groups would you say you like the least?

a. Atheists	b. Homosexuals	c. Muslims	d. Fascists	e. Communists

Considering the group that you picked in the question above, do you agree or disagree with the feeling that members of that group	Agree strongly	Agree somewhat	Disagree somewhat	Disagree strongly
7. should be *banned from being president*?	a.	b.	c.	d.
8. should be *allowed to teach* in public schools?	a.	b.	c.	d.
9. should be *allowed to make a speech* in your city/town?	a.	b.	c.	d.
10. should *have their phones tapped* by our government?	a.	b.	c.	d.
11. should be *outlawed*?	a.	b.	c.	d.

12. In general, would you say that *most* of what government does makes things better or worse for people?

a. *Most* of what government does makes things better for people.	b. *Most* of what government does makes things worse for people.	c. Don't know.

13. Within our culture there exist theories that challenge the historical record or the consensus among the scientific community, such as the notion that the moon landing was fake, that global warming is a myth, that there was a conspiracy to assassinate JFK, and that the US government staged the September 11 attacks. Which of the following describes your views of these theories that challenge the historical record or the consensus among the scientific community?

a. I believe many of these theories.	b. I believe one or two of these theories.	c. I don't believe any of these theories.

14. Do you agree or disagree with the statement: People like me don't have any say about what the government does?

a. Agree strongly	b. Agree somewhat	c. Neither agree nor disagree	d. Disagree somewhat	e. Disagree strongly

15. Do you FAVOR or OPPOSE the death penalty?

a. Favor	b. Oppose	c. Don't know

We'd like to get your feelings about some groups in American society using a version of what is called a feeling thermometer. Using the thermometer to the right how would you rate	0° very cold or unfavorable feeling	cold or unfavorable feeling	50° neutral	warm or favorable feeling	100° very warm or favorable feeling
16. Muslims	a.	b.	c.	d.	e.
17. Blacks / African Americans	a.	b.	c.	d.	e.
18. Undocumented immigrants	a.	b.	c.	d.	e.
19. Homosexuals	a.	b.	c.	d.	e.

20. Over the years, how much attention do you feel the government pays to what people think when it decides what to do? The government

a. ALWAYS pays attention to what people think.	b. USUALLY pays attention to what people think.	c. SOME-TIMES pays attention to what people think.	d. RARELY pays attention to what people think.	e. NEVER pays attention to what people think.

Have you done any of the following during your life?

21. Voted in a presidential primary election in 2008 or participated in a caucus.	a. yes	b. no
22. Written a letter/email to or called a public official.	a. yes	b. no
23. Worked on a political campaign.	a. yes	b. no
24. Volunteered or worked in a government or political official's office.	a. yes	b. no
25. Watched a political debate.	a. yes	b. no
26. Contributed money to a political campaign.	a. yes	b. no
27. Attempted to convince someone to vote a certain way.	a. yes	b. no
28. Been part of an organization that involves itself in politics in some way, such as environmental groups, gun rights groups, student organizations that deal with politics, etc.	a. yes	b. no

29. Ultimately, how do you think historians will view the George W. Bush administration?

a. Very favorably	b. Somewhat favorably	c. Neither favorably nor unfavorably	d. Somewhat unfavorably	e. Very unfavorably

30. For whom did you vote in the November 2008 presidential election?

a. McCain	b. Obama	c. Other	d. I did not vote

31. Do you agree or disagree with the following statement: The best way to deal with the threat of terrorism is to hunt down and kill all the terrorists.

a. Agree strongly	b. Agree somewhat	c. Disagree somewhat	d. Disagree strongly

32. Would you regard the use of torture against people suspected of involvement in terrorism as acceptable or unacceptable?

a. Acceptable	b. Unacceptable	c. No opinion

We are interested in finding out what people think about the Harry Potter books and the movies. Please answer the following questions on the Harry Potter series.

33. How many of the Harry Potter books have you read?

a. None of them	b. Some of them	c. All of them

34. Regardless of whether you have read the books, have you discussed the books with any good friend or family member who read them?

a. Yes	b. No

35. With regard to the Harry Potter book series, did your parents

a. encourage you to read the books or read them with/to you?	b. not really play any role in your decision whether to read the books?	c. discourage you from reading the books?

36. How many of the Harry Potter MOVIES did you see?

a. None of them	b. Some of them	c. All of them

37. Regardless of whether you have seen the movies, have you discussed the MOVIES with any good friend or family member who saw them?

a. Yes	b. No

38. On the scale below where "a" represents a fans who are/were very much into the Harry Potter series and "e" people who haven't read/seen any of the series or, if they did, hated it, where would you place yourself?

a. Was or is into the *Harry Potter* books and/or movies	b.	c.	d.	e. Not a fan / did not read books or watch movies

If you did not read the books, please skip to question number 41

39. At about what grade level did you start to read the books (or have them read to you)?

a. Prior to 4th grade	b. 4th to 6th grade	c. 7th to 9th grade	d. 10th to 12th grade	e. College or later

40. Which of the following best describes the effect of the Harry Potter book series on your reading habits?

I was not much of a reader until I read the Harry Potter series, but after reading Harry Potter, I began to read more books.	I was not much of a reader until I read the Harry Potter series, and after reading Harry Potter I still wasn't much of a reader of books.	I was an avid reader even before I read the Harry Potter series.

The following questions cover your knowledge of the series. If you haven't read the books or seen the movies, please skip to question 46

41. Who is the Half Blood Prince?

a. Severus Snape	b. Harry Potter	c. Voldemort	d. Draco Malfoy	e. I don't know

42. Who is Peeves?

a. Professor of Muggle studies	b. Harry's secret crush	c. A troublesome poltergeist at Hogwarts	d. Dumbledore's phoenix	e. I don't know

43. What is Ron's position in Quidditch?

a. Seeker	b. Keeper	c. Chaser	d. Beater	e. I don't know

44. Which of the magical spells wards off Dementor attacks?

a. Alohomora	b. Avada Kedavra	c. Expecto Patronum	d. Stupefy	e. I don't know

45. The vanishing cabinet connects Hogwarts to

a. Malfoy's mansion	b. The Shrieking Shack	c. The Hog's Head	d. Borgin & Burke's	e. I don't know

Finally, please answer the following questions about yourself.

46. What year are you in school?

a. 1st	b. 2nd	c. 3rd	d. 4th	e. 5th or more (including graduate school)

47. Are you a political science major or minor?

a. Yes	b. No

48. Please indicate your gender.

a. Female	b. Male	c. Transgendered

49. Please tell us your age.

a. 17–18	b. 19–20	c. 21–22	d. 23–25	e. 25 or above

50. How would you characterize the place you grew up?

a. In a large city	b. In suburbia	c. In a small city	d. In a rural area

51. Outside of the books you were assigned for school, what kind of reader were you when you were younger?

a. I was not much of a reader of books.	b. I was an occasional reader of books.	c. I was an avid reader of books.

52. What race do you consider yourself?

a. White	b. Black or African American	c. American Indian or Alaska Native	d. Asian	e. Of mixed race or some other race

53. Do you consider yourself Hispanic or Latino(a)?

a. Yes	b. No	c. I am part Hispanic/Latino(a)

54. Which of the following best describes your father's education?

a. He stopped after high school or before.	b. He attended some college and/or earned an Assoc. degree.	c. He earned a B.A. or B.S. degree.	d. He earned a professional degree.	e. I don't know.

55. How prestigious did you think your father's job was when you were about 16?

a. Very prestigious	b. Somewhat prestigious	c. Not prestigious at all	d. My father was not employed.	e. I don't know.

56. Please indicate the number of times you were spanked as a child.

a. Never spanked	b. Spanked once	c. Spanked on occasion	d. Spanked frequently

57. Generally speaking do you consider yourself a Democrat, Republican, Independent, or other?

a. Democrat	b. Republican	c. Independent	d. Other	e. Don't know

Please whether you agree or disagree with the following statements	Strongly agree	Agree somewhat	Neutral	Disagree somewhat	Strongly disagree
58. I am a productive person who always gets the job done.	a	b	c	d	e
59. I have a wide range of intellectual interests.	a	b	c	d	e
60. I don't feel like I'm driven to get ahead.	a	b	c	d	e
61. If I feel my mind starting to drift off into daydreams, I usually get busy and start concentrating on some work or activity instead.	a	b	c	d	e
62. I find philosophical arguments boring.	a	b	c	d	e
63. I would rather keep my options open than plan everything in advance.	a	b	c	d	e

64. When it comes to politics, do you usually think of yourself as very liberal, liberal, moderate or middle of the road, conservative, or very conservative?

a. Very liberal	b. Liberal	c. Moderate	d. Conservative	e. Very conservative

Regression Analyses

Tables C.1 and C.2 follow on pages 98–101.

TABLE C.1
Regression Results for Full Sample

Independent variables	Feeling thermometer score	Intolerance	Authoritarian predisposition	Reader	Open to experience
	Dependent variables				
HP books read	.11	−.13	−.05	.37	.05
Authoritarianism	−.14	.18			
Race	−.03	.01			
Male	−.06				
City	.06	−.00			.02
UVM	.01	−.01			
Reader			−.05		.10
Open to experience			−.09		
Father's education			−.05	.07	
Ideology					−.15
Partisan					
Political science major					
Cynicism					
Internal political efficacy					
Feeling thermometer					.
Republican					
R-square	.10	.06	.05	.18	.08

Notes: UVM = University of Vermont. Shaded cells are significant at the .05 level or better, one-tailed test. This table reports the OLS regression coefficients for the analyses discussed in chapter 4. All measures were standardized to range between 0 and 1 before entering into the analysis. See text for a description of the creation of the variables and appendix B for the question wordings.
* Significant at the .10 level, one-tailed test.

			Dependent variables				
Ideology	Cynicism	Internal political efficacy	Participation scale	Skepticism	History judge Bush negatively	Vote Obama 2008	Oppose violence
−.15	−.08	.05	.04	.07	.03*	.12	.08
							−.10
.04							
−.04							
−.07							
	−.08						
					−.29	−.71	−.37
	−.02	.07	.04				
		.07					
			−.00				
			.18	.12			
							.54
					−.11	−.37	
.08	.05	.04	.06	.02	.20	.29	.32

TABLE C.2
Regression Results for Those Who Were Not Encouraged to Read the Harry Potter Books

Independent variables	Feeling thermometer score	Intolerance	Authoritarian predisposition	Ideology
	Dependent variables			
HP books read	.09	−.11	−.07	−.14
Authoritarianism	−.13	.18		
Race	−.03	.02		
Male	−.06			.04
City	.05	−.01		−.03
UVM	.01	.00		−.08
Reader			−.03	
Open to experience			−.08	
Father's education			−.05	
Ideology				
Partisan				
Political science Major				
Cynicism				
Internal political efficacy				
Feeling thermometer				
Republican				
R-square	.09	.05	.05	.08

Note: Shaded cells are significant at the .05 level or better, one-tailed test.
* Significant at the .10 level, one-tailed test.

			Dependent variables			
Cynicism	Internal political efficacy	Participation scale	Skepticism	History judge Bush negatively	Vote Obama 2008	Oppose violence
−.09	.04	.05	.08	.01	.11	.05*
						−.11
−.06						
				−.34	−.76	−.35
−.01	.08	.04				
	.07					
		−.01				
		.20	.18			
						.58
				−.09	−.35	
.05	.04	.07	.03	.20	.31	.32

Model of Harry Potter Effects with Coefficients

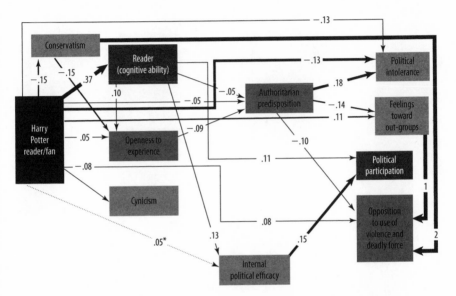

Figure D.1. Direct and indirect effects of Harry Potter with coefficients. Numbers reported are unstandardized regression coefficients (measures were standardized prior to analysis). All coefficients are significant at the .05 level or better. *Relationship without controlling for whether respondent was an avid reader (asked for only half the sample); not significant when readership controlled for (using half the sample).

Introduction · *Isn't It Just a Story?*

1. We use Neil Howe and Bill Strauss's delineation of generations for this research; the Millennial Generation comprises individuals who were born between 1982 and about 1995.

2. BBC, "Harry Potter Finale Sales Hit 11 Million," 23 July 2007, http://news .bbc.co.uk/2/hi/entertainment/6912529.stm, accessed 7 June 2010.

3. Internet Movie Data Base (IMDB), "All-Time Box Office: Worldwide," http:// www.imdb.com/boxoffice/alltimegross?region=world-wide, accessed 12 December 2011.

4. Intercollegiate Quidditch Association, http://collegequidditch.com/index .php?option=com_content&view=article&id=170&Itemid=54, accessed 7 June 2010.

5. Her own discussion of the values she finds important can be found in her Harvard commencement speech in 2009 (http://www.the-leaky-cauldron.org/2008/ 6/5/entire-text-of-j-k-rowling-harvard-commencement-speech-now-online). For a discussion of some of the political aspects of the books, see Barton, "Harry Potter."

6. Scott Keeter, Juliana Horowitz, and Alec Tyson, "Young Voters in the 2008 Election," a PEW Research Center for the People & the Press publication, 12 November 2008, http://pewresearch.org/pubs/1031/young-voters-in-the-2008 -election, accessed 11 June 2012.

7. See the PEW Research Center's report "Millennials: A Portrait of the Next Generation. Confident. Connected. Open to Change," 24 February 2010, http:// pewresearch.org/millennials/, accessed 7 June 2010.

8. *South Park*, episode 1112, "Imaginationland: Episode III," originally aired on 7 March 2007 (emphasis added).

9. Ronald D. Moore, "Mr. Universe," *New York Times*, Op-Ed, 18 September 2006.

10. Gabriel and Young, "Becoming a Vampire"; Sester and Green, "You Are Who You Watch."

11. There is a rich and growing literature on the impact of the news on the public through mechanisms such as agenda setting, priming, and framing, but, to the best of our knowledge, these concepts and the efforts of the political science community have infrequently been applied to the entertainment media (though one might argue that in the US system there is no difference between the news media and the entertainment media since they are both designed to amuse in order to reap a profit).

12. Feldman and Sigelman, "Political Impact"; Lenart and McGraw, "America Watches *Amerika*"; Delli Carpini and Williams, "Constructing Public Opinion"; Baumgartner and Morris, "*Daily Show* Effect."

13. See Perse, *Media Effects*, for a summary of media effects research.

14. On authoritarian predisposition, we draw from Karen Stenner's work detailed in *Authoritarian Dynamic*.

15. Rowling, *Order of the Phoenix*, 810.

16. "Children and Watching T.V.," American Academy of Child and Adolescent Psychiatry's Facts for Families no. 54, http://www.aacap.org/cs/root/facts_for_families/children_and_watching_tv, accessed 6 December 2011.

Chapter 1 · The Subtle (and Not-So-Subtle) Political Lessons of Harry Potter

1. Rowling, *Sorcerer's Stone*, 102.
2. Ibid., 108–9.
3. Rowling, *Deathly Hallows*, 10–11.
4. Ibid., 488–89.
5. Rowling, *Sorcerer's Stone*, 78.
6. Ibid., 80.
7. Rowling, *Chamber of Secrets*, 150.
8. Rowling, *Order of the Phoenix*, 127.
9. Rowling, *Goblet of Fire*, 224–25.
10. Rowling, *Chamber of Secrets*, 62.
11. Rowling, *Deathly Hallows*, 11–12.
12. Ibid., 241–42.
13. See Adorno et al., *Authoritarian Personality*.
14. Stenner, *Authoritarian Dynamic*, 33.
15. Rowling, *Order of the Phoenix*, 239.
16. Ibid.
17. Ibid., 213–14.
18. Ibid., 265.
19. Rowling, *Sorcerer's Stone*, 118. Emphasis added.
20. Rowling, *Goblet of Fire*, 119.
21. Rowling, *Half-Blood Prince*, 497–98.
22. Ibid., 498.
23. Rowling, *Deathly Hallows*, 573–74.

24. Ibid., 70–71.
25. Rowling, *Sorcerer's Stone*, 65.
26. Rowling, *Goblet of Fire*, 708.
27. Rowling, *Order of the Phoenix*, 93–94.
28. For more on the portrayal of government in the series, see Barton, "Half-Crazed Bureaucracy."
29. Rowling, *Goblet of Fire*, 304–5.
30. Rowling, *Deathly Hallows*, 129–31.

Chapter 2 · Learning the Lessons of the Wizarding World

1. See Perse, *Media Effects*.
2. Incidental learning is not considered entirely passive even though it is considered a passive learning approach; see Anderson, *Cognitive Psychology*.
3. Gerbner et al., "Growing Up with Television."
4. There is a label for the belief that the media affects others more than yourself: it is what is known as the "third person effect"; see Mutz, "Influence."
5. Jennings and Niemi, *Political Character of Adolescence*, 15. This process is also covered by social learning theory; see Bandura, *Social Foundations*.
6. Jennings, Stoker, and Bowers, "Politics across Generations."
7. Campbell, *Why We Vote*; Gimpel, Lay, and Schuknecht, *Cultivating Democracy*; Conover and Searing, "Political Socialization Perspective."
8. Romer, Jamieson, and Pasek, "Building Social Capital."
9. The students who helped designed the interview project and conduct the interviews included Daniel Albert, Louis Armistead, Marta Ascherio, Jesse Brady-Searby, Chantal Champaloux, Erica Deitrick, William Dunnack, David Eitler, Joshua Fredman, Kevin Haar Jr., Vanessa Jump, Matthew Kiernan, Meghan Krezinski, Tracey MacKenzie, Kensington Moore, and Joseph Thomas.
10. Some conservative Christian groups actively discourage their members from reading the Harry Potter series.
11. See Slater, "Reinforcing Spirals."
12. *24* is television series that follows the actions of a special agent fighting terrorist threats to the United States.
13. Student interview, 2011, in Seger, "Harry Potter."
14. Student interview, 2011, in Seger, "Harry Potter."
15. Dawson, Prewitt, and Dawson, *Political Socialization*; Tedin, "Influence of Parents"; Jennings and Niemi, "Transmission of Political Values."
16. Mannheim, "Problem of Generations."
17. Ibid.
18. Student interview, 2011, in Seger, "Harry Potter."
19. For a discussion of this social learning process, see Bandura, "Social-Learning Theory," and Carpenter and Green, "Flying with Icarus."
20. Sester and Green, "You Are Who You Watch," 276.
21. Gabriel and Young, "Becoming a Vampire."

22. For example, see Sester and Green, "You Are Who You Watch," and Gabriel and Young, "Becoming a Vampire."

23. Perse, *Media Effects and Society*, 195.

24. Mannheim, "Problem of Generations."

25. Ibid., 379.

26. It is an underidentified statistical model because the number of endogenous variables in the model (age, year, and generation) outnumber the possible number of exogenous variables (age and year).

27. Howe and Strauss, *Millennials Rising*; Winograd and Hais, *Millennial Momentum*.

28. Howe and Strauss, *Millennials Rising*.

29. Scott Keeter, Juliana Horowitz, and Alec Tyson, "Young Voters in the 2008 Election," PEW Research Center for the People & the Press, 12 November 2008, http://pewresearch.org/pubs/1031/young-voters-in-the-2008-election, accessed 11 June 2012.

30. The class was my spring 2008 Integrated Social Sciences Program (ISSP) American Political System course at the University of Vermont. The students were Marlee Baron, Kelvin Chen, Danielle DeGrandis, Jason Depatie, Timothy Douglas, Jaime Dusseault, Amanda Fox, Matthew Gibbs, Colin Henkel, Michael Lamb, Anna Lavenberg, Kathryn Marshall, Briana Martin, Matt McKeon, Max McNamara, Gus Melita, Ryan Mueller, Ally Perleoni, Abigail Reiber, Janell Schafer, Jesse Simmons, and Megan Tonelli.

31. See, for example, Howe and Strauss, *Millennials Rising*, and Winograd and Hais, *Millennial Momentum*.

32. Class research project, ISSP American Political System, University of Vermont, spring 2008.

33. National Endowment for the Arts (NEA), "To Read or Not to Read: A Question of National Consequence," Research Report 47, November 2007, http://www.nea.gov/research/toread.pdf, accessed 22 November 2011, 7.

34. Ibid., 10.

35. Donald F. Roberts, Ulla G. Foehr, and Victoria Rideout, "Generation M: Media in the Lives of 8–18 Year-olds," Kaiser Family Foundation Study, Henry J. Kaiser Family Foundation, March 2005, http://www.kff.org/entmedia/upload/Generation-M-Media-in-the-Lives-of-8-18-Year-olds-Report.pdf, accessed 23 November 2011; NEA, "To Read or Not to Read."

36. Cunningham and Stanovich, "What Reading Does for the Mind."

37. Stenner, *Authoritarian Dynamic*.

38. NEA, "To Read or Not to Read"; Romer, Jamieson, and Pasek, "Building Social Capital."

39. NEA, "To Read or Not to Read," 6.

40. Ibid., 48.

41. Ibid.

42. Roberts, Foehr, and Rideout, "Generation M."

43. Discussion of the methodology used for these interviews can be found in appendix A.

44. Student interviewed in class research project, Film, TV and Public Opinion, University of Vermont, 2010.

45. Student interview, 2011, in Seger, "Harry Potter."

46. This parallels my experience, as I only became a reader after being introduced to J. R. R. Tolkien's *The Hobbit* and the Lord of the Rings trilogy.

Chapter 3 · Do the Politics of Harry Potter Fans Reflect Those of the Wizarding World?

1. The names of all the students who were involved in this project are listed in the front of this book.

2. Many thanks to Rick Travis and David Breaux at Mississippi State, Robert Brown at the University of Mississippi, and my colleagues at the University of Vermont.

3. Many thanks to Wendy Johnston at Adirondack Community College, Matt Moore and Anika Leithner at Cal Poly, Matt Potowski at Iowa State, and Stephen Woolworth at Pacific Lutheran.

4. ANOVA, F = 25.5, significant at the .000 level.

5. Pearson correlation coefficients between feeling thermometer scores and each measure of fandom, self-placement on a Harry Potter (HP) fan scale, the sum of the correct trivia questions, and the number of HP books read, were .13, .15, and .20, all statistically significant.

6. Average feeling thermometer score was 13.5 for those who saw all the movies and a 13.0 for those who did not (ANOVA, F = 5.0, significance level .025).

7. We used a modified version of the measure developed by John L. Sullivan, James Piereson, and George E. Marcus (see *Political Tolerance*).

8. In choosing the groups, we tried to provide different dimensions in order to provide a diversity of choices so that the measure would come as close as possible to Sullivan, Piereson, and Marcus's measure.

9. Pearson correlation coefficients between the level of intolerance and each measure of fandom, self-placement on HP fan scale, the sum of the correct trivia questions, and the number of HP books read, were, −.09, −.17, −.18, all statistically significant. The average intolerance score for those who saw all the movies was 5.7, it was 6.1 for those who did not (F = 3.8, significance level of .048).

10. Correlations between responses to the question on equality and score on trivia questions was .08, it was .10 for the fan scale (both statistically significant at the .05 level or better). Those who saw all the movies were also more likely to support greater equality (difference of means, statistically significant).

11. Political socialization paper of "Film, TV and Public Opinion" student, 2009.

12. This is a derivation of the measure of authoritarianism used by Stenner, *Authoritarian Dynamic*, and Feldman and Stenner, "Perceived Threat." As Stenner

did with her college sample, the measure was converted from one that asked respondents about their preferred child rearing practices to one that simply asks respondents to choose the preferred word (since child rearing questions would not be appropriate for most college-aged respondents).

13. Pearson correlation coefficients were –.13 for the fan scale and –.20 for the trivia questions (both significant at the .01 level).

14. Margin of error at the 95% confidence level is ±2.9 percentage points.

15. Margin of error at the 95% confidence level is ±2.9 percentage points.

16. Questions 12, 13, and 19 in the survey (see appendix B).

17. On the ANES internal political efficacy question (question number 14), 56% of fans and 48% of nonfans scored high.

18. ANOVA of differences of means for cynicism, $F = 16.0$, significance level .000, for participation, $F = 7.0$, significance level at .008.

19. Scott Keeter, Juliana Horowitz, and Alec Tyson, "Young Voters in the 2008 Election," PEW Research Center for the People & the Press, 12 November 2008, http://pewresearch.org/pubs/1031/young-voters-in-the-2008-election, accessed 11 June 2012.

20. Margin of error at the 95% confidence level is ±2.9 percentage points.

Chapter 4 · The Role of Harry Potter in the Political Development of Millennials

1. Stenner, *Authoritarian Dynamic.*

2. Stenner calls those opposite of authoritarians "libertarians."

3. Stenner, *Authoritarian Dynamic.*

4. Student interview, 2011, in Seger, "Harry Potter."

5. Student paper, Film, TV and Public Opinion, University of Vermont, 2009.

6. Student paper, Film, TV and Public Opinion, 2009.

7. Student interview, 2011, in Seger, "Harry Potter."

8. Ibid.

9. Stenner, *Authoritarian Dynamic.*

10. Research has found the father's level of education—not the mother's—to be an important control variable for the authoritarian predisposition. This is because the father's education level is related to strict child-rearing practices that are, in turn, related to levels of the authoritarian predisposition.

11. Student paper, Film, TV and Public Opinion, 2009.

12. Student interview, 2011, in Seger, "Harry Potter."

13. See Perse, *Media Effects.*

14. As measured by how many of the Harry Potter books they read or by their self-placement on the Potter fans scale.

15. These would involve estimating an equation for why individuals became fans in the first place (a statistical way of controlling for self-selection into fandom) and testing the model using structural equation modeling. We did not ask enough questions that would allow us to estimate an equation for selection.

16. Student paper, Film, TV and Public Opinion, 2009.

17. Student paper, Film, TV and Public Opinion, 2009.

18. Student paper, Film, TV and Public Opinion, 2009.

19. Student paper, Film, TV and Public Opinion, 2009.

20. Student paper, Politics and the Media, University of Vermont, 2010.

21. Student paper, Politics and the Media, 2010.

22. Student paper, American Political System, University of Vermont, 2011.

23. Student paper, Political Science Honors Seminar, University of Vermont, 2011.

Conclusion · *Fiction, Reality, and Politics*

1. Hively and Eveland, "Contextual Antecedents."

2. Unless your book club is the Thursday night book club at the Three Penny Tap Room.

3. Student interview, 2011, in Seger, "Harry Potter."

Adorno, Theodor, Else Frenkel-Brunswik, Daniel J. Levinson, and R. Nevitt San-
ford. *The Authoritarian Personality*. New York: Harper & Row, 1950.

Anderson, John R. *Cognitive Psychology and Its Implications*. New York: W. H.
Freeman, 1995.

Ball-Rokeach, Sandra, and Melvin DeFleur. "A Dependency Model of Mass Media
Effects." *Communications Research* 3 (1974): 3–21.

Bandura, Albert. *Social Foundations of Thought and Action: A Social Cognitive
Theory*. Englewood Cliffs, NJ: Prentice-Hall, 1986.

———. "Social-Learning Theory of Identificatory Processes." In *Handbook of
Socialization Theory Research*, edited by David A. Goslin. Chicago: Rand Mc-
Nally, 1969.

Barton, Benjamin H. "Harry Potter and the Half-Crazed Bureaucracy." *University
of Michigan Law Review* 104 (2006): 1523–38.

Baumgartner, Jody, and Jonathan S. Morris. "The *Daily Show* Effect: Candidate
Evaluations, Efficacy, and American Youth." *American Politics Research* 34
(2006): 341–67.

Campbell, David E. *Why We Vote: How Schools and Communities Shape Our Civic
Life*. Princeton, NJ: Princeton University Press, 2006.

Carpenter, Jordan M., and Melanie C. Green. "Flying with Icarus: Narrative
Transportation and the Persuasiveness of Entertainment." In *The Psychology of
Entertainment Media: Blurring the Lines between Entertainment and Persua-
sion*, edited by L. J. Shrum. New York: Routledge, 2012.

Conover, Pamela Johnston, and Donald D. Searing. "A Political Socialization Per-
spective." In *Rediscovering the Democratic Purposes of Education*, edited by
Lorraine M. McDonnell, P. Michael Timpane, and Roger Benjamin. Lawrence:
University Press of Kansas, 2000.

Cunningham, Anne E., and Keith E. Stanovich. "What Reading Does for the
Mind." *Journal of Direct Instruction* 1 (2001): 137–49.

Dawson, Richard E., Kenneth Prewitt, and Karen S. Dawson. *Political Socialization*. New York: Little, Brown, 1977.

Delli Carpini, Michael X., and Bruce A. Williams. "Constructing Public Opinion: The Uses of Fictional and Nonfictional Television in Conversations about the Environment." In *The Psychology of Political Communication*, edited by Ann N. Crigler. Ann Arbor: University Michigan Press, 1996.

Feldman, Stanley, and Lee Sigelman. "The Political Impact of Prime-Time Television: 'The Day After.'" *Journal of Politics* 47 (1985): 556–78.

Feldman, Stanley, and Karen Stenner. "Perceived Threat and Authoritarianism." *Political Psychology* 18 (1997): 741–70.

Gabriel, Shira, and Ariana F. Young. "Becoming a Vampire without Being Bitten: The Narrative Collective-Assimilation Hypothesis." *Psychological Science* 10 (2011): 1–5.

Gerbner, George, Larry Gross, Michael Morgan, and Nancy Signorielli. 2002. "Growing Up with Television: The Cultivation Perspective." In *Media Effects: Advances in Theory and Research*, edited by J. Bryant and D. Zillmann. Hillsdale, NJ: Lawrence Erlbaum Associates, 43–68.

Gimpel, James G., J. Celeste Lay, and Jason E. Schuknecht. *Cultivating Democracy: Civic Environments and Political Socialization in America*. Washington, DC: Brookings Institution Press, 2003.

Hively, Myiah Hutchens, and William P. Eveland Jr. "Contextual Antecedents and Political Consequences of Adolescent Political Discussion, Discussion Elaboration, and Network Diversity." *Political Communication* 26 (2009): 30–47.

Howe, Neil, and William Strauss. *Millennials Rising: The Next Great Generation*. New York: Vintage Books, 2000.

Jennings, M. Kent, and Richard G. Niemi. *The Political Character of Adolescence: The Influence of Families and Schools*. Princeton, NJ: Princeton University Press, 1974.

———. "The Transmission of Political Values from Parent to Child." *American Political Science Review* 62 (1968): 169–84.

Jennings, M. Kent, Laura Stoker, and Jake Bowers. "Politics across Generations: Family Transmission Reexamined." *Journal of Politics* 71 (2009): 782–89.

Lenart, Silvo, and Kathleen McGraw. "America Watches 'Amerika': Television Docudrama and Political Attitudes." *Journal of Politics* 51 (1989): 697–712.

Mannheim, Karl. "The Problem of Generations." In *From Karl Mannheim*, 2nd expanded ed., edited by Kurt H. Wolff. New Brunswick, NJ: Transaction Publishers, 1993.

Mutz, Diana C. "The Influence of Perceptions of Media Influence: Third Person Effects and the Public Expression of Opinions." *International Journal of Public Opinion Research* 1 (1989): 3–23.

Perse, Elizabeth M. *Media Effects and Society*. Mahwah, NJ: Lawrence Erlbaum Associates, 2001.

Romer, Daniel, Kathleen Hall Jamieson, and Josh Pasek. "Building Social Capital in Young People: The Role of Mass Media and Life Outlook." *Political Communication* 26 (2009): 65–83.

Rowling, J. K. *Harry Potter and the Chamber of Secrets.* New York: Scholastic, 1999.

———. *Harry Potter and the Deathly Hallows.* New York: Scholastic, 2007.

———. *Harry Potter and the Goblet of Fire.* New York: Scholastic, 2000.

———. *Harry Potter and the Half Blood Prince.* New York: Scholastic, 2005.

———. *Harry Potter and the Order of the Phoenix.* New York: Scholastic, 2003.

———. *Harry Potter and the Prisoner of Azkaban.* New York: Scholastic, 1999.

———. *Harry Potter and the Sorcerer's Stone.* New York: Scholastic, 1997.

Sapiro, Virginia. "Not Your Parents' Political Socialization: Introduction for a New Generation." *Annual Review of Political Science* 7 (2004): 1–23.

Seger, Julie. "Harry Potter and the Millennial Generation's Politics." Honors thesis, University of Vermont, 2011.

Sester, Marc, and Melanie C. Green. "You Are Who You Watch: Identification and Transportation Effects on Temporary Self-Concept." *Social Influence* 5 (2010): 272–88.

Shrum, L. J., and Jaehoon Lee. "The Stories TV Tells: How Fictional TV Narratives Shape Normative Perceptions and Personal Values." In *The Psychology of Entertainment Media: Blurring the Lines Between Entertainment and Persuasion,* edited by L. J. Shrum. New York: Routledge, 2012.

Slater, Michael D. "Reinforcing Spirals: The Mutual Influence of Media Selectivity and Media Effects and Their Impact on Individual Behavior and Social Identity." *Communications Theory* 17 (2007): 281–303.

Stenner, Karen. *The Authoritarian Dynamic.* Cambridge: Cambridge University Press, 2005.

Stone, William F., and Paul E. Schaffner. *The Psychology of Politics.* 2nd ed. New York: Springer-Verlag, 1988.

Strauss, William, and Neil Howe. *The Fourth Turning: An American Prophecy.* New York: Broadway Books, 1997.

Sullivan, John L., James Piereson, and George E. Marcus. *Political Tolerance and American Democracy.* Chicago: University of Chicago Press, 1993.

Tedin, Kent L. "The Influence of Parents on the Political Attitudes of Adolescents." *American Political Science Review* 68 (1974): 1579–92.

Winograd, Morely, and Michael D. Hais. *Millennial Momentum: How a New Generation Is Remaking America.* New Brunswick, NJ: Rutgers University Press, 2011.